Desserts

James Martin

Desserts

a fabulous collection of recipes from
Sweet Baby James

photography by Peter Cassidy

QUADRILLE

This edition first published in 2010 by Quadrille Publishing Limited
Alhambra House, 27–31 Charing Cross Road, London WC2H 0LS

Reprinted in 2011, 2012, 2013
10 9 8 7 6 5 4

Editorial director: *Jane O'Shea*
Creative director: *Helen Lewis*
Editor and project manager: *Gillian Haslam*
Art direction and design: *Gabriella Le Grazie*
Photography: *Peter Cassidy*
Food styling: *Chris Start, Lisa Harrison* and *Bridget Sargeson*
Props styling: *Wei Tang*
Production: *Vincent Smith, Bridget Fish*

British Library Cataloguing-in-Publication Data
A catalogue record for this book is available from the British Library.

ISBN: 978 184400 947 3

Printed in China

Contents

Introduction

This is the book I've been wanting to write for over a decade. It's a compilation of all my favourite desserts, including recipes that have been in my family for generations, classic dishes, traditional favourites that I've given a new twist to, plus lots of recipes that I've developed from scratch. The desserts range from warming, comfort food such as sticky toffee pudding (how can anyone resist that?) and white chocolate, whisky and croissant pudding, to light, summery dishes such as apple or mango sorbet and raspberry puff pastry stack. There are homely puds, including individual apple and blueberry pies and spicy plum crumble, and the classics found on many restaurants menus – lemon tart, chocolate profiteroles, even Black Forest gâteau which deserves a new lease of life. There are cakes and bakes you can put together in a matter of minutes, plus celebration cakes such as the white chocolate wedding cake and the stunning fire-and-ice cake.

This book has developed from a television series, *Sweet Baby James*, which I filmed in various places around the UK. While on my travels for the show, I visited Lucy's deli and restaurant in Ambleside in the Lake District. There she holds a monthly pudding night called 'Up The Duff Night', serving just puddings to all the diners. I say 'puddings' as in 'more than one' – I was actually served six, one after another. They all arrived at the table hot and loaded with cream. First was a clotted cream rice pudding, rich and creamy with the skin on the top (just how it should be) to prove it had been cooked in the oven and not subjected to the microwave. Next up was a rhubarb crumble, again with cream,

followed by a banana fruit cake pud, also hot and served with cream. At this point my belt gave way to my belly and I had to call it a night, but the 12 women I was with battled on with another three puds.

These pudding-only nights are nothing new in the US – New York eateries serving only desserts are opening all the time, and the trend is spreading to Europe. It just goes to prove real puddings hold a special place in our hearts and many fond memories. They can either remind you of school dinners or mum's or gran's special dessert surprise. The Hot Puddings chapter is full of these classics and modern twists on dishes that have been around for years. There are dishes like peach Melba that's been given the modern chef treatment but still retains all the elements that combine to make it such a great dish. I've also simplified troublesome dishes such as the soufflé – everyone's nightmare dinner party dish, but when it's made with bought-in custard I promise you can't fail. In the Tarts and Flans chapter, you'll find apple pie – the nation's favourite pudding – served with blueberries, the new super fruit according to the healthy eating experts, plus many other ideas for both new and old pastry-based dishes.

All households used to have a baking day only some years back, but now it's sad to see so many people resorting to buying the plastic-coated, dried rubbish from the supermarket. The art of baking isn't a science; it's one of knowledge and practice, and if you were to ask chefs what they remember of their childhood food, homemade cakes and biscuits would come up in the conversation. I know they would in mine. That's why I love visiting the WI stalls at fairs and shows around the UK – they bring back so many great memories of my gran and auntie who were both amazing pastry cooks. None of my family were chefs, just great cooks, and that's why we can learn something by just visiting these cake stalls selling great food cooked with love by a generation who really understand the art of good baking. Take a look at the Cakes and Bakes chapter where you'll find plenty of recipes to tempt you into baking again.

The Cold Puddings chapter is for all those people who come up to me to say the reason for not making desserts is the lack of time. The chapter is full of stuff you can make in advance and even leave in the freezer for a week or two. There are desserts you can take your time over in order to get them right as well as simpler ones to make in minutes. It's the same with many of the recipes in the Ice Creams and Sorbets chapter – most of them can be made in advance.

If you want to learn the real art of true cooking, you start at the beginning. Many people think pastry is a science, but it's all about understanding the basics and knowing why things do what they do. For me, it's where my passion for cooking first began. As a young kid, I'd watch my gran rubbing butter and flour together in a bowl balanced on her knees while she watched a whole episode of *Coronation Street*, always listening to the show but never distracted from the task in hand. Her pastry was better then any pastry I've ever tasted since, and that's down to the way the fat was incorporated into the flour. You wouldn't think that a small thing like that would make such a difference, but it does. Follow my recipes in the Basics chapter, and you, too, can master the not-so-difficult task of pastry-making.

So flick through the pages in this book – you're guaranteed to find plenty to tempt you back into the kitchen.

Basics

Rich shortcrust pastry

1 Mix together the flour and salt (and icing sugar if making sweet pastry). Add half the cubed butter to the flour. Gently and swiftly, rub the fat into the flour until it resembles coarse breadcrumbs. Add the rest of the butter and mix until it's the size of small peas. Make a well in the centre of the dry ingredients.

2 Mix the egg with the lemon juice and water and pour into the well a little at a time, rubbing it through your fingers, until it forms a dough (you may not need all the liquid). Turn onto a floured board and knead lightly until smooth. Shape into a ball, wrap in clingfilm and refrigerate for at least 30 minutes before rolling out.

3 To line a tin or mould, roll the chilled pastry onto the rolling pin, then unroll over the tin, draping the pastry into the tin or mould. Gently press it in place using your fingers.

MAKES 300G

200g plain flour

¼ tsp salt

2 tbsp icing sugar (if making sweet pastry)

100g cold unsalted butter, cubed

1 egg, beaten

1 tsp lemon juice

2 tbsp iced water

The best way to make shortcrust with that crumble-in-the-mouth texture is to do it by hand rather then by machine, as a blender will overwork the gluten in the flour and cause the pastry to be springy and shrink when cooked. In addition, resting the pastry in the fridge is important, as the high proportion of butter to flour makes it difficult to roll out when warm. Any unused pastry can be frozen (freeze it rolled into a tin, rather than in a ball).

Simple rough puff pastry

1 Mix together the flour and salt. Cut the butter into small cubes (this is where the recipe differs from flaky pastry – see page 18) and mix the butter into the flour without breaking up the lumps. Mix to a stiff dough with 100ml cold water and the lemon juice.

2 On a floured board, roll the dough into a rectangle three times as long as it is wide – about 30 x 10cm.

3 Fold the top third down and bottom third up. Turn the pastry sideways and seal the edges. Continue to roll and fold four times, leaving the pastry to rest for 15 minutes between each folding and rolling. Wrap in clingfilm and leave to rest and chill in the fridge for 30 minutes before using.

MAKES 350G

200g plain flour

¼ tsp salt

150g butter

1 tsp lemon juice

Until ready-made all-butter puff pastry is more widely available in the shops, this is the recipe you need for great-tasting puff pastry.

Choux pastry

1 Pre-heat the oven to 220°C/425°F/ Gas mark 7. Put 125ml water, the milk, diced butter, salt and caster sugar in a saucepan set over a high heat and boil for 1 minute, stirring with a spatula. Turn off the heat and, stirring all the time, quickly add the flour until the mixture is very smooth.

2 When the mixture is smooth, replace the pan over the heat and stir with the spatula for 1 minute. The paste will begin to poach and some of the water will evaporate. Don't let the paste dry out too much, or it will crack during cooking. Immediately add the eggs off the heat, one at a time, mixing in with a spatula.

3 Stir well with the spatula until the eggs are thoroughly combined and the paste has a very smooth texture. It is now ready to use.

MAKES 24 PROFITEROLES OR
16 ECLAIRS

125ml milk

100g butter, cut into small pieces

3g fine salt

5g caster sugar

150g flour, sifted

4 medium eggs

There are two golden rules when making choux pastry. The first is the method – you need to cook the flour for about a minute until you can hear a slight popping sound in the pan, then allow to cool before adding the eggs. The second concerns baking the pastry – place a baking tray in the bottom of the oven and just before closing the oven door, throw half a cup of water into the bottom of the oven.

4 Carefully spoon the mixture into a large piping bag fitted with a plain 1cm nozzle.

5 Pipe out the paste onto baking parchment or a greased baking tray. Smooth down any bumps on the piped pastry with a finger dipped in water. Pipe small buns if making profiteroles or longer shapes for eclairs.

6 Place the baking tray in the oven, then throw half a cup of water onto the oven floor to create some steam. Bake in the oven, opening the oven door slightly (about 1–2cm) after 5 minutes and leave it ajar. Cooking time will vary from 10–20 minutes, depending on the size of the buns or eclairs.

This will create steam to start the rising of the choux. However, too much steam will cause the choux to collapse, so open the oven door for a few seconds about 5 minutes into the cooking time to allow some steam to disperse.

Old-fashioned flaky pastry

This is a really simple method for making flaky pastry, and if you make a bit more than you need, it freezes really well. It tastes far better than the bought-in stuff. The use of lard adds an old-fashioned taste to the pastry, which is great for topping savoury pies and traditional desserts to give that 'just-as-granny-used-to-make' taste.

MAKES ABOUT 470G

200g plain flour

¼ tsp salt

75g butter, softened

75g lard, softened

1 Sieve the flour and salt into a large bowl. In a separate bowl, mix together the butter and lard and divide into four equal portions. Rub one of these portions into the flour and mix to a soft dough with 150ml water.

2 Roll this pastry into a rectangle three times as long as it is wide, measuring 30 x 10cm. Dot another quarter of the fat over the top two-thirds of the rolled-out pastry. Fold the bottom third up and the top third down. Turn the dough sideways. Press down the edges of the pastry to seal the fat inside. Roll out again and leave the pastry to rest in the fridge for 10 minutes

3 Repeat this procedure until all the fat is used up, resting the pastry for 5 minutes between each turn. Wrap in clingfilm and leave to chill in the fridge for at least 30 minutes.

4 When ready to use, roll out on a lightly floured surface (not too much flour as this will toughen up the pastry) to a thickness of 3mm. If the pastry starts to warm up and become sticky at any time, wrap it in clingfilm and chill for about 15 minutes before continuing.

Victoria sponge

1 Pre-heat the oven to 190°C/375°F/ Gas mark 5. Grease and flour two 20cm sandwich tins. Place the butter, caster sugar and vanilla essence into a bowl or blender and mix well to a creamy consistency.

2 Then slowly mix the eggs into the bowl, adding them one by one.

3 Fold in the flour. When mixed, pour into the tins and bake for 20–25 minutes until well risen and golden brown. The cakes should spring back when pressed on top with a finger. Turn out and leave to cool on wire racks.

MAKES TWO 20CM CAKES

200g butter, plus extra for greasing

200g caster sugar

½ tsp vanilla extract

200g self-raising flour

4 medium eggs

Named after Queen Victoria, this sponge cake can be made by two different methods, each using the same basic ingredients. One method is to mix the eggs and sugar together first as in a Génoese (see page 20), the other method (featured here) is to cream the butter and sugar together like a bun mixture. You get two very different results, but for a lighter cake I would go for this method. I think the best taste comes from the creaming method but I will leave the choice to you, and happy baking.

Génoese sponge

This is a classic cake recipe and the butter gives the cake a slightly longer shelf-life and a touch more moisture. Mix the eggs and sugar well before adding the rest of the ingredients. Once the flour and butter are added, work quickly to fold them in so that the cake doesn't lose its aeration. Great served with whipped cream, jam and a dusting of icing sugar.

MAKES ONE 22CM SPONGE

6 medium eggs

175g caster sugar

175g plain flour, sifted

50g butter, melted

1 Pre-heat the oven to 200°C/400°F/Gas mark 6. Grease and flour a 22cm sponge tin and line the base of the tin with greaseproof paper.

2 Place the eggs and sugar into a bowl and whisk until the mixture has doubled in volume and reached the ribbon stage (this means the mixture trails like ribbons from the whisk). This will take a few minutes.

3 Fold the sifted flour into the mixture carefully but quickly, adding the melted butter at the same time.

4 Pour into the tin and bake in the oven for 30–35 minutes. Test with a skewer in the centre, and if it comes out clean, the sponge is ready. Allow to cool in the tin for 10 minutes before turning out.

Chocolate cake

These are the two different methods I use for chocolate cake. If you want to keep the cake for a few days, use the second method as the addition of butter will help moisten the cake and prevent it drying out.

BOTH RECIPES MAKE TWO
20CM CAKES

butter, for greasing

6 medium eggs, separated

150g caster sugar

50g cocoa powder, sifted

1 Pre-heat the oven to 180°C/350°F/Gas mark 4. Lightly butter two 20cm cake tins and line the bases with greaseproof paper

2 Place the eggs yolks and sugar into a clean bowl and whisk well with a hand whisk for 2–3 minutes, then add the cocoa powder.

3 In a larger bowl, whisk the whites until firm, then carefully fold them into the egg yolk mixture.

4 Pour the mixture into the cake tins, level the top with a palette knife and bake for about 15 minutes. Remove from the oven and allow to cool slightly before turning out onto wire racks.

175g butter, softened

175g sugar

½ tsp vanilla extract

3 medium eggs

100g self-raising flour

1 tsp baking powder

25g cocoa powder

1 Pre-heat the oven to 170°C/340°F/Gas mark 3½. Lightly butter two 20cm cake tins and line the bases with greaseproof paper.

2 Place the butter, sugar and vanilla extract in a bowl and whisk for 4–5 minutes until light and fluffy. Add the eggs – they must be added one at a time or the mixture will split.

3 Sieve the flour, baking powder and cocoa over the mixture and carefully fold in with a spatula. Pour into the two tins.

4 Bake in the oven for 30–35 minutes. Remove from the oven and allow to cool slightly before turning out onto wire racks.

Tuiles

Most professional pastry cooks will have this raw mixture waiting in the fridge, ready to make into a dessert or to decorate a cake. It's so versatile to use. Just don't let the biscuits colour too much in the oven or they can taste bitter. Remember to work quickly when the tuiles come out of the oven as you don't have long to mould them into shapes before they firm up.

MAKES APPROXIMATELY
24 DIFFERENT SHAPES

115g unsalted butter, softened

140g icing sugar, sifted

3 egg whites

115g plain flour

1 Pre-heat the oven to 200°C/400°F/Gas mark 6. Create a template by cutting a hole of the desired shape and size in the lid from a margarine tub.

2 Cream the butter and sugar together. Slowly add the egg whites to the mix, and then fold in the flour at the end.

3 Place your template on a baking tray lined with a non-stick baking mat. Spread the tuile mix very thinly over the hole with a palette knife, then lift off the template, leaving a perfect shape. Repeat to make as many tuiles as required.

4 Bake in the oven for 4–5 minutes until lightly coloured around the edges. Leave the tuiles to cool flat, or bend over an eggcup or something similar in size if you want a shape. Leave until cold.

5 To make the 'snake' shape, place the mixture in a piping bag fitted with a small plain nozzle. Pipe the mixture into the desired shape onto the lined baking tray. Bake as above. When baked but still warm, carefully remove the tuile from the baking tray and place over a curved object (such as a rolling pin or bottle) and leave to cool.

Shortbread

The secret of making good shortbread is to mix the dough as little as possible and to chill it after mixing as the high content of butter will not allow you to roll it out straight away. I often find the best way to cook it is in a low oven, so that it bakes without colouring too much. For citrus-flavoured shortbread (as used in the lemon curd syllabub on page 85), add the zest of 2 lemons or oranges in step 1.

MAKES 16–20

225g chilled unsalted butter, plus extra for greasing

225g flour, plus extra for dusting

60g caster sugar, plus extra for dusting

pinch of salt

½ vanilla pod, seeds only

1 Dice the butter and put it into a mixing bowl to soften. Sift the flour on top with the caster sugar, a pinch of salt and the vanilla seeds. Rub together gently and form into a ball. Alternatively, blitz all the ingredients in a food processor until they come together into a ball.

2 Lightly flour the work surface, then roll out the shortbread mixture until it is about 5mm thick. Prick all over the surface with a fork.

3 Using a sharp knife, cut the shortbread into fingers measuring about 5cm in length and about 1.5cm wide. Carefully lift onto a baking tray and rest in the fridge for 30 minutes or so.

4 Pre-heat the oven to 180°C/350°F/Gas mark 4. Dust the shortbread with a little caster sugar before baking. Bake for 20 minutes, or until golden brown and firm to the touch. Leave until completely cooled before removing from the baking tray.

Brandy snaps

The uncooked mixture can be stored in the fridge for up to a week and then baked when needed. If the brandy snaps firm up too quickly while you are using them, place them back in the oven for a few minutes and they will soften up.

MAKES ABOUT 35

100g caster sugar

pinch of ground ginger

50g unsalted butter, softened, plus extra for greasing

50g plain flour

50g golden syrup

1 Place the sugar, ginger and butter in a bowl and slightly cream together. Add the flour and golden syrup and mix to a firm paste.

2 Roll into a long sausage about 3.5cm in diameter and then wrap tightly in clingfilm. Chill well (overnight is best).

3 Pre-heat the oven to 180°C/350°F/Gas mark 4. Lightly grease a baking tray or use a non-stick baking mat.

4 Remove the clingfilm from the mixture and cut into slices 5mm thick. Arrange the slices on the baking tray, spacing them out well. Bake for about 8-10 minutes, or until well spread out and golden. Remove from the oven and leave to cool for a few seconds to firm up slightly.

5 Using a palette knife or fish slice, carefully remove one brandy snap at a time from the baking tray and then immediately wrap it loosely around the handle of a wooden spoon to shape into a roll (if the brandy snaps cool too quickly and start to break, replace the baking tray in the oven for a minute or so to soften them up again slightly). Once shaped, leave to cool.

6 Slide the cooled brandy snaps off the spoon handles and store in an airtight container. I love mine filled with whipped cream.

Cinder toffee honeycomb

1 Place the sugar, honey and glucose in a heavy-based pan with 100ml water. Place the pan on the heat and, using a sugar thermometer, bring to the boil and boil to 160°C/325°F (a light caramel).

2 Grease a large baking tray with oil while the sugar is boiling. When the pan reaches the required temperature, remove from the heat, quickly add the bicarb and whisk in speedily.

3 Working quickly, pour the mixture onto the tray – it will start to bubble up quite dramatically straight away. Leave to cool. When cold, break up and mix with ice cream, or to make hokey pokey, dice into chunks and coat in dark chocolate.

400g caster sugar

100ml runny honey

2 tbsp liquid glucose

oil, for greasing

1½ tsp bicarbonate of soda

200g dark chocolate, melted (optional)

Cinder toffee (also called honeycomb) is the stuff you've probably always wanted to know how to make. The secret is to work quickly once the bicarb has been whisked in. It's great scattered over ice cream or broken into pieces and coated in chocolate, which I would call hokey pokey.

Chocolate ganache

This is a basic ganache to which you can add different flavourings, such as rum, brandy, yuzu (see page 60) or maccha (a strong, powdered Japanese green tea – use 1 tsp, and don't be tempted to substitute leaf tea). If you add more chocolate, the mix will become firmer when cold. You can either shape the ganache into truffles, or use it as a chocolate filling for cakes and desserts (this recipe makes enough to fill and top a 30cm cake).

MAKES 36 TRUFFLES

275g dark chocolate, minimum 60% cocoa solids, broken into pieces

50g unsalted butter, at room temperature

250ml double cream

4 tbsp rum (if making truffles)

50g cocoa powder (if making truffles)

1 Place the chocolate and butter in a large bowl. Bring the cream to the boil and pour it over the chocolate and butter. Stir gently until the chocolate has melted, trying not to create bubbles. If making truffles, stir in the rum.

2 Place the bowl of ganache in the fridge to firm up, removing it about 15 minutes before you want to use it.

3 If making truffles, put the cocoa into a bowl. Ensure your hands are cold and dry, then dust them with cocoa. Take spoonfuls of the ganache mixture (use a teaspoon or a tablespoon) and roll the mixture into a ball in your cocoa-dusted hands. Drop each truffle into the bowl of cocoa, turn it around and then toss it between your palms to remove any excess powder. The truffles can be returned to the fridge and kept for up to 2 days as long as they are stored in an airtight container.

Praline

1 Heat the sugar in a non-stick pan. Make sure the sugar dissolves and the colour is a nice caramel (the praline can taste bitter if it colours too much). Pour the almonds into the caramel and stir quickly.

2 Pour the mixture onto a non-stick mat or onto a sheet of greaseproof paper on a baking tray to cool. Spread the praline out to a thickness of about 1cm.

3 When the praline has set, lightly crush with a rolling pin or break into shards to serve. It can be stored in an airtight container.

MAKES 20 SERVINGS

150g caster sugar

100g toasted flaked almonds

This is a great partner to chocolate, walnut and coffee desserts and can be used in so many ways. Use small shards on ice cream, or blend in a food processor to a sand-like dust to sprinkle over desserts. It's also fantastic sprinkled in a fine layer onto a non-stick baking mat on a baking tray and baked at 180°C/350°F/Gas mark 4 for 4–5 minutes, then cut into shapes while still warm to create fine biscuits – very cheffy I know, but it looks fab.

Chocolate curls

1 Melt the chocolate in a heatproof bowl set over a saucepan of barely simmering water (make sure the base of the bowl doesn't touch the water). When the chocolate has melted, pour it onto a flat, smooth surface to a thickness of about 5mm.

2 Smooth the chocolate over the surface using a stepped palette knife. Leave the chocolate to set – what you want is for the chocolate to be set hard enough so that if you press the surface it doesn't leave an indentation. Don't be tempted to try to speed up the cooling process by placing the chocolate in the fridge, as this will cause it to crack when rolling the curls.

3 Use a wallpaper scraper or pastry scraper to make the curls (a knife will do if you hold the blade in both hands). Pull it along the chocolate towards you and it should curl up (or work away from you if it's easier). If it doesn't curl and you end up with a pile of chocolate shavings they'll look just as nice – either way, place them in a plastic container and store in the fridge until required.

300g dark chocolate (70–75%cocoa solids), broken into squares

There is no real art to this other than using a scraper and waiting for the chocolate to set just right. Too warm and nothing will happen; too cold and you will need a chisel rather than a scraper. I'm afraid it's just a case of practice and trial and error. I like to use a warm, clean oven tray. The tray can be warmed in the oven or with a cook's blowtorch. If the tray has a lip all around, it's easier to use it upside down. As a guide, 300g of dark chocolate will enable you to make enough curls to decorate a 20cm cake. The curls also look good dusted with cocoa powder.

Spun sugar

1 Place the sugar in a very clean, non-stick pan and place on the heat. Do not stir. When the sugar starts to turn into a caramel, tilt the pan to mix the sugar as it starts to turn so it blends together. When all the sugar is at a caramel colour and has dissolved, remove the pan from the heat and place the base of the pan in cold water to cool. Don't allow any water in the pan. As the sugar cools, it will become thicker and resemble golden syrup. If it thickens too much, gently reheat.

2 To make spirals, take a tablespoon of sugar and quickly twirl the sugar trail around a cook's steel. Snap off the tail of the sugar and carefully slide the spiral off the steel. Place on a baking tray to set.

3 To make spun sugar, take a tablespoon of the sugar and spin it very quickly backwards and forwards over a cook's steel or a rolling pin. Quickly lift the sugar up and scoop into a bundle. Place on a baking tray to set.

100g white caster sugar

Spun sugar is a great way to decorate desserts (see the photo on page 8), but you will end up with a kitchen covered in the stuff. Just remember to put loads of newspaper all over the floor, light fittings and the pets because at first it will go everywhere. The most important thing in sugar work is the temperature – too hot and nothing will happen; too cold and the sugar will snap.

4 To make pulled sugar, take a tablespoon of the sugar and allow it to fall off the spoon. Pinch the sugar trail between your thumb and forefinger (it will be hot!). Working quickly, pinch two or three strands on top of each other. Snap off the sugar trail when you have made a small bundle. Place on a baking tray to set.

5 To make a basket, grease a small glass bowl or ladle with olive oil (don't use vegetable oil as it's too thin). Take a tablespoon of sugar and criss-cross the mould with the sugar trail.

6 Leave the sugar to set on the mould, then carefully lift the basket off and fill with your chosen dessert, such as ice cream or sorbet.

Use a clean pan, clean sugar (no tea and coffee stains), don't stir the sugar, be patient and have a mop ready for when you've finished – I have warned you! It's best to use plain white refined sugar for this, as organic or light brown caster sugar aren't really 'clean' enough in colour.

Hot meringue

These are the three different methods for making meringue. Each recipe adds the sugar to the egg whites in a different way, but they all make similar meringue. Whichever method you choose, if you prefer a sticky meringue (such as for a pavlova), add a tablespoon of cornflour or white vinegar once the sugar has been added before being baked.

MAKES 1 PAVLOVA, 1 BAKED
ALASKA OR 10 MERINGUE
NESTS

350g white caster sugar

6 egg whites

1 Pre-heat the oven to 200ºC/400ºF/Gas mark 6. Pour the sugar onto a baking tray and place in the oven to warm up.

2 When the sugar has been in the oven for 5 minutes, beat the egg whites in an electric mixer until stiff. Take the sugar out of the oven.

3 When the egg whites are well-risen and firm, set the mixer to the lowest speed and gently pour on the hot sugar in a thin stream, taking no more than 2 minutes to add all the sugar. The meringue is now ready to use.

Cold meringue

MAKES 1 PAVLOVA, 1 BAKED
ALASKA OR 10 MERINGUE
NESTS

6 large egg whites

250g white caster sugar

1 Pre-heat the oven to 140ºC/275ºF/Gas mark 1. Line a baking tray with baking parchment or a non-stick baking mat.

2 Place the egg whites in a large clean bowl and, using an electric whisk on a low speed, begin whisking. Continue for about 2 minutes until the whites are foamy, then switch the speed to medium and carry on whisking until the egg whites reach the stiff peak stage. Next, whisk the sugar in on high speed, a dessertspoon at a time, until you have a stiff and glossy mixture.

3 Spoon the mixture onto the baking tray and place in the centre of the oven and leave it for 1 hour. Turn the oven off and leave the meringues to dry out in the oven until completely cold.

Italian meringue

1 Pour 80ml water in a pan, then add the sugar and glucose, if using. Place over a moderate heat and stir the mixture until it boils. Skim the surface and wash down the sugar crystals which form inside the pan with a brush dipped in cold water. Now increase the heat so that the syrup cooks rapidly. Insert the sugar thermometer to check the temperature.

2 When the sugar reaches 110°C/225°F, beat the egg whites in an electric mixer until stiff. Take the sugar off the heat when it reaches 121°C/250°F.

3 When the egg whites are well-risen and firm, set the mixer to the lowest speed and gently pour on the cooked sugar in a thin stream, taking care not to let it run onto the whisks. Continue to beat at low speed until the mixture is almost completely cold – this will take about 15 minutes. The meringue is now ready to use.

MAKES 1 PAVLOVA, 1 BAKED
ALASKA OR 10 MERINGUE NESTS

360g white caster sugar

30g glucose (optional)

6 egg whites

The smoothest meringue comes from the Italian method (also called boiled meringue) as the boiling sugar cooks the whites when added. It does take a lot of whisking, but it's worth the effort.

Glacé fruits

I first saw these being made in a bakery in France when I was there on work experience from college. The fruits are steeped in sugar syrup for several days, but require very little effort to make.

pineapple, peeled, sliced and
  then quartered

cherries, pitted but kept whole

firm pears, peeled cored and halved

plums, stoned and halved

apricots, stoned and halved

granulated sugar

1 Place all the fruit into a pan and just cover with water, bring to the boil and simmer gently until soft but slightly firm.

2 For each 500g of fruit allow 350ml of syrup. Make this by combining 250ml of the water in which the fruits were cooked with 200g sugar. Stir over a low heat until the sugar has dissolved.

3 Place the cooked fruit in a single layer in a shallow dish and pour over the warm syrup. Cover the dish and leave for 24 hours.

4 The next day, drain the syrup from the fruit and measure into a pan. Add 30g sugar for each 300ml of syrup and bring to the boil. Pour over the fruit, cover and leave for 24 hours. Repeat this twice times – each time adding an additional 40g of sugar to the syrup.

5 On the fifth day, drain the fruit, return the syrup to the pan and add 100g sugar for each 250ml of syrup. Bring to the boil, add the fruit and boil for 2 minutes. Return to the dish and leave for 12 hours. Then repeat this step. The syrup should be like thick honey.

6 Drain the syrup and arrange the fruit in a single layer on a wire rack set over a baking sheet. Leave to dry. Store in an airtight box between layers of waxed paper.

Dried fruit slices

1 Turn the oven to its lowest setting. Line a baking tray with a silicone cooking liner. Using a sharp knife, cut the fruit into wafer-thin slices (only pineapples and mangoes need to be peeled). Don't halve and stone peaches, plums, mangoes, etc – slice until you reach the stone, then turn the fruit around and slice the other side. Apples and pears are best cored neatly, although if sliced thinly enough you can leave the core in.

2 For the stock syrup, place the sugar in a pan with 400ml water and heat slowly until the sugar has dissolved, then cool. Dip the fruits that are prone to discoloration into a little sugar syrup mixed with a squeeze of lemon juice as soon as you slice them.

3 Shake off any excess syrup and lay them in neat rows on the trays. Leave in the oven for 2 hours, turning them once or twice during cooking. If the fruit starts to brown, the oven is too warm. To lower the temperature, prop the door open with the handle of a wooden spoon. The slices are ready when they feel firm and can be lifted off easily. Don't leave them in the oven for longer than is necessary as they crisp up on cooling.

any fruits of your choice, such as apples, pineapple, bananas, mangoes, strawberries, pears or plums

FOR THE STOCK SYRUP:

200g caster sugar

squeeze of lemon juice

These are quite a 'cheffy' thing to make, but they do make the cake or the dessert you put them on look fab. Store the slices in airtight plastic containers. If properly dried, they will keep crisp for at least a week.

Crêpes

I've worked with some chefs who say you should rest the batter after mixing, while others say the opposite. For me, the real secret of a good pancake or crêpe is, firstly, not to make the batter too eggy. Secondly, make it quite liquid and not too thick as this will enable the mixture to spread more quickly and thinly into the pan. Always fry in butter too (never in olive oil or other oils) as it adds to the flavour, and because of the quick cooking the butter will also add colour to the crêpe. See the following pages for sauces to serve with the crêpes, or serve with cream or ice cream.

MAKES 12–16

125g plain flour

2 good pinches of salt (optional)

1 large egg

1 tbsp melted butter, plus extra for frying

300ml milk

1 Place the flour and salt in a bowl and add the egg, melted butter and half the milk. Whisk until smooth and creamy, then mix in the remaining milk.

2 Leave the batter to rest for 10 minutes if you wish, although this is no longer deemed to be necessary as flours are now so thoroughly refined.

3 Heat a pancake pan (approximately 20cm) over a high heat and grease with a knob of butter. Ladle the batter in, swirling to coat the base of the pan and cook the crêpes for 1–2 minutes on each side, until golden.

4 You should get about 12–16 if you make thin ones. Add your choice of filling and cream, ice cream or sauce and serve.

5 If you are making these in advance, layer them with squares of greaseproof and place in the freezer. To serve, defrost and reheat either by placing in a pan with a touch of butter, microwaving for a couple of seconds or heating in the oven for 1 minute at 200°C/400°F/Gas mark 6.

Chocolate sauce

I use sugar syrup here as it makes the sauce less sweet than a mixture of double cream and butter. It also gives the sauce a lovely smooth finish and a shine to it. Don't use a chocolate too high in cocoa, as it will make the sauce bitter. Choose one between 50 and 70 per cent.

MAKES 350ML

15g butter

50g caster sugar

250g good-quality plain chocolate, broken into pieces

25ml brandy or rum (optional)

1 Place the sugar in a pan with 50ml water. Place a bowl on top of the pan and add the broken chocolate and butter.

2 Place onto the heat and bring the water to a simmer with the bowl of chocolate melting on the top.

3 Once the chocolate has melted, remove the bowl from the heat. By then the sugar should have formed a syrup in the pan.

4 Using a spoon, mix the sugar syrup into the chocolate and butter. Stir in the rum or brandy, if using.

5 Serve straight away. The sauce will thicken up if left to go cold, so add a little hot water to loosen it before serving.

Cinnamon sauce

This is the strangest recipe in the book, using goat's milk and baking powder. I don't know what happens to it when boiled but it makes such a great sauce. And before you try it with another type of milk, let me tell you it doesn't work – trust me, I've tried. It will keep in the fridge for about a week and will only need warming up to serve. It's fab with vanilla ice cream.

MAKES 400ML

600ml goat's milk

200g caster sugar

80ml golden syrup

2 cinnamon sticks

1 tsp baking powder

1 Put the milk, sugar and the golden syrup in a pan. Bring to the boil. Crumble the cinnamon sticks into the milk and add the baking powder.

2 Take the pan off the heat and stir well as the mix will rise quickly. Continue to whisk the mixture until it stops rising, then place back on the heat and bring back to the boil, whisking all the time.

3 Turn down the heat and cook for about 45 minutes, simmering, and stirring occasionally to prevent the mixture from burning. It should have the thickness of double cream and be caramel in colour.

Raspberry sauce

1 To make the sauce, simply tip the raspberries and the sugar into a blender with 50ml water and purée well until smooth.

2 Place a sieve over a bowl and pour the blended purée through.

3 Use a spatula to press the sauce through if necessary. Store the sauce in a covered container in the fridge and use as required.

MAKES 150ML

250g fresh raspberries
2 tbsp icing sugar

There are two ways to make this sauce. One method is to cook the berries in the sugar and water which will give you more sauce, but to me it tastes like jam. I much prefer this second method as it has an improved colour and a far better flavour (however, it will produce a little less sauce than the other method). Don't add too much water as it will cause the sauce to split when spooned onto the plate.

Fresh custard

Crème anglaise means English custard, and this doesn't mean the glow-in-the-dark yellow stuff. The most important thing is to make sure the mixture doesn't boil when the eggs are added. You need to heat it up just enough to cook the eggs. The custard is ready when it coats the back of a wooden spoon. You could also mix it with a whisk when the bubbles start to disappear, then pass through a sieve as soon as possible.

MAKES 750ML

8 egg yolks

75g caster sugar

300ml milk

300ml double cream

1 vanilla pod, split

1 Beat the egg yolks and sugar together in a bowl until well blended.

2 Place the milk and cream in a saucepan. Split and scrape the inside of the vanilla pod into the milk and cream and bring to the boil.

3 Once the milk and cream are boiling, pour a little onto the eggs and mix well, then pour back into the pan. Return to the heat and using a whisk, lightly stir the mix to thicken; do not boil.

4 As the egg yolks warm, the cream will thicken to create a custard. Keep stirring until it coats the back of the spoon. Remove from the heat and pass through a sieve and leave to cool. The custard can now be served warm or stirred occasionally until it cools.

Sticky gingerbread pudding

This basic recipe also works well if you use other spices such as cinnamon or nutmeg in place of the ginger.

SERVES 6

140g stem ginger in syrup (8 pieces)

175g self-raising flour

1 level tsp ground ginger

½ level tsp ground cinnamon

½ level tsp ground cloves

1 level tsp baking powder

1 level tsp bicarbonate of soda

2 eggs

75g butter, softened, plus extra for greasing

110g molasses sugar

1 tbsp black treacle

1 heaped tsp freshly grated ginger

175g Bramley apples, peeled, cored and chopped small

1 Pre-heat the oven to 180°C/350°F/Gas mark 4. Grease six 175ml ovenproof pudding basins.

2 Place the pieces of stem ginger in a food processor and turn on the motor for about 7–10 seconds. Be careful not to process for too long – the ginger should be chopped small, but not puréed.

3 Sift the flour, spices, baking powder and bicarbonate of soda into a mixing bowl. Then add the eggs, butter, sugar and treacle. The best way to measure treacle is to grease the spoon first and, using a spatula or another spoon, push it into the bowl to join the rest of the ingredients.

4 Add the freshly grated ginger, then, using an electric hand whisk, whisk everything together gradually, adding 150–175ml warm water until you have a smooth mixture. Finally, fold in the stem ginger and apple.

5 Divide the mixture between the buttered pudding basins, filling them three-quarters full. Stand them on a solid baking sheet and bake in the centre of the oven for 35 minutes, or until they feel firm and springy to the touch.

6 Remove them from the oven and let them stand for about 5 minutes, then run a small palette knife around the edges of the tins and turn them out.

7 Allow the puddings to get completely cold and keep them wrapped in clingfilm until you need them. To reheat, microwave for 1 minute or warm in the oven at 180°C/350°F/Gas mark 4 for 5 minutes.

Hot puddings

Croissant butter pudding

I don't really like the term 'trademark dish', but this is probably the recipe I owe most of my career to. It was the dish that got me noticed at Antony Worrall Thompson's restaurant where it was invented out of necessity – instead of ordering three dozen croissants, 33 dozen were delivered. As a 17-year-old pastry chef, I had to find a way to use them up. It's also the dish that got me spotted in television and led to my first head-chef job when I was 21. The secret is not to over-cook the pudding. It should be quite liquid in the centre because it uses whole eggs and extra egg yolks. It must be made on the day – never place it in the fridge, otherwise it will have to be sliced rather than spooned.

SERVES 4

500ml milk

500ml double cream

1 vanilla pod

3 whole eggs

6 egg yolks

200g caster sugar

6 large croissants

25g sultanas

25g butter, melted

175g white chocolate, cut into shards

75ml whisky

icing sugar, for dusting

Pre-heat the oven to 180°C/350°F/Gas mark 4.

Pour the milk and cream into a pan, add the vanilla pod, and gradually bring to the boil.

Place the eggs, egg yolks and sugar in a food mixer bowl and mix gently using the whisk attachment on a low setting.

While the cream is heating, slice the croissants and place in an ovenproof dish, slightly overlapping the pieces. Sprinkle with sultanas and pour over the butter.

Once the cream has boiled, take it off the heat. Add the egg mixture and chocolate and stir well. Place to one side off the heat to allow the chocolate to melt, stirring occasionally.

Add the whisky to the cream mixture. Using a sieve, strain the cream over the croissants and bake in the oven for 20–25 minutes or until almost set.

Remove from the oven and dust with icing sugar. Caramelize the topping using a very hot grill or, if you have one, a blowtorch. This is best served at room temperature, with a spoonful of ice cream.

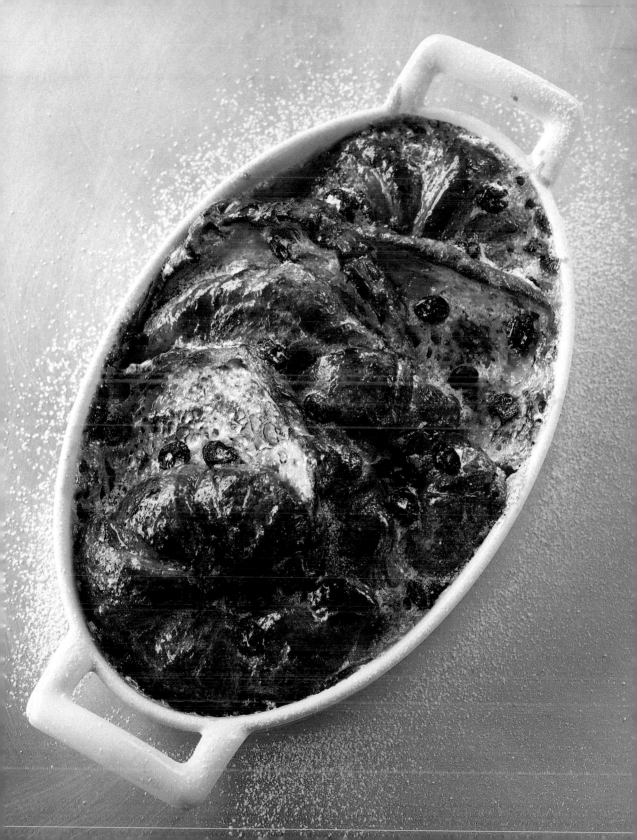

Apple and blueberry pie

The combination of apple and blueberries makes a wonderful, slightly sharp pie filling. Make sure the apples are not overcooked – if they are cooked for too long in the pan, by the time you place them in the pie and cook them again you will end up with a fine purée. Aim for delicate chunks of soft apple so that the pie filling has some texture. If you would prefer to make one large pie, use a 22cm pie dish and cook for 25–30 minutes.

SERVES 6

450g shortcrust pastry (see page 14)

flour, for dusting

550g cooking apples, such as Bramleys

100g caster sugar, plus extra for sprinkling

finely grated zest and juice of ½ a lemon

150g blueberries

25g butter

1 egg, beaten

clotted cream or ice cream, for serving

Pre-heat the oven to 200°C/400°F/Gas mark 6. Grease six 7.5cm dariole moulds.

Roll out two-thirds of the pastry on a floured work surface and cut out circles slightly larger than the moulds. Line the greased moulds with pastry.

Peel, quarter and core the apples, then slice them thickly into a bowl with three-quarters of the sugar, the lemon juice and zest. Stir gently to mix.

Heat a pan and add the apples with the butter and remaining sugar. Cook for 3–4 minutes, then add the blueberries. Cook for a few more minutes, then remove from the heat and cool.

When cool, fill the pastry-lined moulds with the filling.

Roll out the remaining pastry approximately 1cm larger than the moulds and place it on top of the filling. Seal the edges well and then make a small hole in the top to allow the steam to escape.

Make decorations from any pastry trimmings (I like to make a few leaves) and seal them with a little water. Brush the tops of the pies with beaten egg, then dust with caster sugar. Bake for 15 minutes until the fruit is tender and the top is golden brown. Serve hot with clotted cream or ice cream.

Passion fruit and custard soufflé

This is my foolproof way for cooking soufflés – it works every time for me. The secret is to use ready-made custard, not the glow-in-the-dark, fluorescent type made by mixing powder with milk. Buy fresh, good-quality custard from a supermarket or good delicatessen and combine it with egg whites and flavourings. I use passion fruit, adding the pips as they add a light, delicate flavour. I serve it with sautéed bananas and a scoop of vanilla ice cream on the side – the two flavours go particularly well. If you want to alter the flavour, adding citrus zest or juice will change it to a lemon or orange soufflé.

SERVES 4

50g butter

3 tbsp caster sugar

4 medium egg whites

1 passion fruit, halved

8 tbsp fresh ready-made custard

2 medium bananas

vanilla ice cream, to serve

Pre-heat the oven to 180°C/350°F/Gas mark 4. Grease four ramekins using half the butter and dust the insides with 1 tbsp of the caster sugar.

Whisk the egg whites in a bowl until stiff, then add 1 tbsp of the caster sugar.

Scoop the passion fruit into the custard, and then gently fold in the whisked egg whites. Spoon the mixture into the prepared ramekins and place on a baking tray. Bake for 15–20 minutes.

While the soufflés are cooking, peel the bananas and cut in half lengthways.

Heat up a non-stick pan and add the remaining butter. When it's nut-brown in colour, add the remaining sugar and the halved bananas. Fry them on both sides until they are a nice golden colour, taking care not to break them up.

To serve, place the warm bananas on the plate, the soufflé on the side and, if you dare, a dollop of vanilla ice cream too!

Spicy plum crumble

This is a dish that anybody can make. While filming the television series, we made this crumble with a group of city bankers. They were surprised just how easy it was. To be honest, you can make a crumble without even cooking the filling simply by chopping apples and adding a few blackcurrants or something similar, placing the crumble mixture on top and slowly baking in the oven for 25–30 minutes. This recipe is quicker as the filling is cooked and already hot when placed in the dish, so all you need to do is add the crumble and finish off in the oven. I make this dish quite a lot at home because there are a lot of plum trees in my garden.

SERVES 8

15 fresh dark plums, cut in half and stones removed

50g butter

1 vanilla pod, split

1 star anise

few gratings of nutmeg

2 cinnamon sticks

100ml red wine

5 tbsp golden syrup

4 tbsp caster sugar

FOR THE CRUMBLE:

100g butter, softened

100g demerara sugar

180–200g plain flour

Pre-heat the oven to 200°C/400°F/Gas mark 6.

Sauté the plums with the butter in a hot frying pan for a few minutes. Add the split vanilla pod, star anise, nutmeg and cinnamon, red wine, syrup, sugar and 50ml water, then bring to the boil and simmer gently for 6–8 minutes.

As the plums break down to a thick, syrupy texture, place in an ovenproof dish.

To make the crumble, mix the butter and flour together until the mixture resembles breadcrumbs, then mix in the sugar. Sprinkle the crumble over the plums and bake in the oven for 20–25 minutes or until golden brown.

Remove from the oven and allow to cool slightly before serving with ice cream or double cream.

Classic spotted dick

You cannot have a dessert book without featuring spotted dick and custard. It's usually served with custard, but my grandmother would serve it just with plain butter while my auntie would just sprinkle demerara sugar over the top. The 'spotted' refers to the currants which resemble spots and the 'dick' actually comes from the word 'dough'. It's also known as spotted dog, plum bolster and spotted Richard.

SERVES 8

25g soft butter, for greasing
350g plain flour
2 tbsp baking powder
150g shredded suet
75g caster sugar
150g currants
25g butter, melted
zest and juice of 2 lemons
1 egg
150ml milk
150ml double cream

Butter a piece of greaseproof paper measuring about 60cm square with the soft butter.

Place all the dry ingredients in a bowl, then add the melted butter. Stir in the lemon juice and zest, egg and while stirring slowly add the milk and cream until you reach a dropping consistency.

Spoon the mixture into the paper and roll up into a sausage shape about 6cm in diameter. Don't roll the paper too tight, otherwise the mixture will not rise and be light when cooked.

Tie at the ends with string and place the pudding in a hot steamer, fitted with a lid, and steam for about 1¼ hours until cooked.

Remove the pudding from the steamer and unwrap from the paper, then spoon into the bowls.

Serve with custard (see page 44) or vanilla ice cream (see page 176).

Baked parkin with rhubarb

I remember when my grandmother used to bake parkin. It is traditionally served on Bonfire Night in Yorkshire. It's a fantastic cake and has a similar texture to sticky toffee pudding but it's made with oats and the addition of plenty of golden syrup makes this cake very moist. It gets even better the longer it's kept. Ideally, bake parkin 2–3 days in advance and it will become very sticky all the way through the cake.

SERVES 8

170g self-raising flour

pinch of salt

3 tsp ground ginger

2 tsp nutmeg

1 tsp mixed spice

120g oat flakes

250g golden syrup

75g black treacle

150g unsalted butter, plus extra for greasing

150g soft dark brown sugar

2 medium eggs, beaten

25ml milk

FOR THE SYRUP:

200g golden syrup

100ml apple juice

1 tsp ground mixed spice

4 sticks fresh rhubarb, cut into 5cm lengths

TO SERVE:

vanilla ice cream

fresh mint

Pre-heat the oven to 140°C/275°F/Gas mark 1. Grease a 30 x 20cm cake tin and line with greaseproof paper.

Sieve the flour, salt, ginger, nutmeg and mixed spice together into a large bowl. Mix in the oats.

Place the syrup, treacle, butter and soft brown sugar in a small saucepan and melt over a gentle heat, but do not boil. Stir into the flour mixture.

Mix in the beaten egg and milk to create a soft, almost pouring, consistency. Pour into the buttered tin.

Bake for 1–1¼ hours until firm in the centre. Remove from the oven and leave in the tin for 5–10 minutes before turning out.

Meanwhile, to make the hot spiced syrup, simply whisk all the ingredients together in a small pan and warm, but don't boil. Add the rhubarb and cook gently for 3–4 minutes to soften a little.

Serve the parkin warm, on top of the warm syrup and rhubarb and topped with ice cream. Drizzle over the remaining syrup and serve with a sprig of fresh mint.

Steamed treacle sponge pudding

I collect old English cookbooks dating from the eighteenth century. You can't pick one of them up without looking at the dessert chapter where you will find plenty of steamed sponge puddings – in particular this idea which I class as a 'proper pudding'. This simple dish can be left steaming for several hours. You can also make it in advance and place it in the fridge, then re-steam it or re-heat in the microwave. The most important thing with this dessert is to use really good-quality treacle and proper butter – you'll never get the same flavour using margarine.

SERVES 6–8

3 tbsp golden syrup, plus 3-4 tbsp extra to serve

175g self-raising flour

1 rounded tsp baking powder

175g very soft butter

3 large eggs

175g soft light brown sugar

1 tbsp black treacle

Butter a 1.2 litre pudding basin well. Cut a double thickness of kitchen foil measuring approximately 30 x 40cm.

Grease a tablespoon and measure the 3 tbsp golden syrup into the pudding basin.

Sift the flour and baking powder into large mixing bowl and add the soft butter, eggs, sugar and black treacle. Using an electric hand whisk (or a large fork and a lot of elbow grease), beat the mixture for about 2 minutes or until it has thoroughly blended. Spoon the mixture into the basin and use the back of a spoon to level the top.

Cover the basin with the foil, making a pleat in the centre. Pull the foil down the outside of the basin and tie in place around the rim with string, taking the string over the top and tying it on the other side to make a handle for easy lifting. Trim off the excess foil all the way around.

Place the pudding in a steamer fitted over a saucepan of boiling water and steam the pudding for 2 hours, checking the water level halfway through.

To serve, loosen the pudding all around using a palette knife, invert it onto a warmed plate and pour the extra syrup over the top before taking it to the table. Serve with custard or ice cream.

Fresh orange curd pudding

I love this pudding as it's so simple. If you ever visit a Japanese food store, try to pick up a yuzu – it's a sour Japanese citrus fruit. Yuzu has a mandarin flavour and a tart sharpness like grapefruit. Add a little into this pud instead of the lemon zest and juice for an even better flavour.

SERVES 4–6

300ml fresh orange juice

grated zest and juice of 1 lemon

60g butter, softened, plus extra for greasing

90g caster sugar

4 large eggs, separated

70g self-raising flour

½ tsp baking powder

160ml milk

icing sugar, for dusting

Pre-heat the oven to 180°C/350°F/Gas mark 4. Butter the sides of a 1-litre soufflé dish, or other similar ovenproof dish, and set aside.

Put the orange and lemon juices in a saucepan, bring to the boil and boil until reduced by just over half. Set aside to cool.

In a bowl, beat the butter with the sugar and lemon zest until white and creamy. Mix in the egg yolks, one at a time. Sift the flour and baking powder together over the mixture, then mix to combine.

Slowly add the orange and lemon juice and milk to the mixture, stirring to blend.

Now whisk the egg whites in another bowl until they form stiff peaks. Beat a third of the whisked egg whites into the runny sponge mixture, then carefully fold in the rest using a large spoon.

Stand the prepared dish in a roasting tin, then pour in the mixture. Pour boiling water around the dish to create a bain-marie and place in the oven.

Bake for 50–60 minutes until the pudding is golden brown and firm on top. Cover the dish with foil if the top browns too quickly.

Remove the dish from the oven and dust the pudding with icing sugar before serving.

Sticky toffee pudding with toffee sauce

The origins of sticky toffee pudding are mixed. Some people say it comes from the Sharrow Bay Hotel in the Lake District, while others claim it comes from The Udny Arms Hotel in Aberdeenshire. For me, I like to think Francis Coulson or Brian Sack, the original owners of the Sharrow Bay, invented this dish in their fantastic hotel on the banks of Lake Ullswater. All I've done over the years is to tweak their recipe. I make it with a really rich toffee sauce – let's face it, if you're going to make a pud like this, you've got to do it properly!

SERVES 6–8

75g soft butter

175g dark brown demerara sugar

200g self-raising flour, plus extra for dusting

1 tbsp golden syrup

2 tbsp black treacle

2 eggs

1 tsp vanilla extract

200g pitted dried dates

1 tsp bicarbonate of soda

FOR THE TOFFEE SAUCE:

100g dark soft sugar

100g butter

200ml double cream

Pre-heat the oven to 200°C/400°F/Gas mark 6. Grease a 23cm tin thoroughly with 25g of the butter, then dust the inside of the tin with flour.

Using a food mixer, blend the remaining butter and sugar together. Slowly add the golden syrup, treacle, eggs and vanilla extract to the butter mixture and continue mixing. Turn the mixer down to a slow speed and then add the flour. Once all the ingredients are combined, turn off the mixer.

Place the dates in a saucepan with 300ml water and bring to the boil. Purée the water and date mixture and add the bicarbonate of soda. While it is still hot, quickly add this mixture to the egg mix. Once the mix is combined, pour into the prepared tin and bake for 40–45 minutes until the top is just firm to the touch.

Remove the pudding from the oven and allow to cool, then turn out of the tin and cut into squares.

To make the sauce, melt the butter and sugar together in a small pan, add the cream and bring to the boil. Simmer for a few minutes until the sauce reaches the desired consistency.

To serve, re-heat the sponge in a microwave or heat for 5 minutes in the oven at 180°C/350°F/Gas mark 4. Place onto a plate with lots of the sauce on the top and a scoop of vanilla ice cream if you wish.

The sponge and sauce can be made in advance. The sponge can even be frozen and both can be plated up and re-heated in the microwave.

Pear and lemon verbena crème brûlée

Lemon verbena is a fantastic herb that goes particularly well in this dish and in other desserts such as like crème caramel and most set custards. It's such an easy herb to grow in the garden and produces quite a strong flavour, but it needs to be infused prior to cooking and the leaves drained off as overcooking the leaves can make them taste bitter.

SERVES 6–8

500ml milk

500ml double cream

3 sprigs of lemon verbena,
    finely chopped

7 egg yolks

110g caster sugar

2 poached or tinned pears

55g demerara sugar

Pre-heat the oven to 150°C/300°F/Gas mark 3.

Heat the milk and cream gently in a pan with the chopped lemon verbena. Remove from the heat and allow to cool before blending the mixture with a hand blender.

Place the egg yolks in a bowl, add the sugar and whisk together until pale and thickened.

Add the milk and cream mixture to the egg yolks and whisk well. Pass through a sieve and allow to rest for 10 minutes. Skim off the top layer to remove any foam.

Ladle the mixture into ramekins and place in a roasting tin. Place in the oven and pour in enough hot water to come halfway up the sides of the ramekins. Bake for 1½ hours until set. Remove from the roasting tin and allow to cool. When cool, refrigerate the crème brûlées for 2 hours, until firm.

To serve, drain the pears and cut into thin slices and arrange on the top of the ramekins. When ready to eat, sprinkle the demerara sugar over the top and caramelize either with a blowtorch or by putting them under a hot grill.

Baked Alaska

The secret of this dessert is to bake it in the oven without the ice cream melting. However, using a cook's blowtorch rather than oven baking makes this dessert far easier to prepare. The trick is make sure you pipe plenty of meringue over the surface, then quickly go over it with a cook's blow torch. It's great served with either the raspberry sauce given here or a hot chocolate sauce (see page 42).

SERVES 6–8

1 quantity Italian meringue (see page 35)

FOR THE RASPBERRY SAUCE:

250g raspberries

2 tbsp icing sugar

FOR THE FILLING:

15cm disc of plain sponge

1–2 tbsp brandy

500ml vanilla ice cream

1 punnet strawberries, hulled and cut in halves or quarters

First, make the raspberry sauce by blending the raspberries and icing sugar with 25ml water in a mini food processor until smooth. Pass through a sieve.

Next, make up the Italian meringue following the instructions on page 35.

Place the sponge on a plate and drizzle with 1–2 tbsp brandy. Spoon the vanilla ice cream on top and the strawberries over and around the edge (save a few strawberries to decorate).

Spread the meringue all over using a palette knife to seal in the ingredients. Place the remainder of the meringue in a piping bag fitted with a star nozzle and pipe around the edge and on the top.

Using a cook's blowtorch, glaze the meringue to colour.

Garnish the baked Alaska with the remaining strawberries, drizzle with the raspberry sauce and dive in.

Hot chocolate fondants with summer berries and mint froth

The secret of a good hot chocolate fondant is the liquid centre. I've simplified the recipe by using bought chocolate truffles. If you want to make these for a dinner party, it's best to make them up, freeze them when raw and then flash them in the oven. Give them an extra 5 minutes cooking time when cooked from frozen. The mint froth is simply milk warmed in a pan with crème de menthe. All you need is the froth on the top of the milk.

SERVES 6

190g dark chocolate with at least
  60% cocoa solids

100g butter, softened

35g ground almonds

2 large eggs, separated

35g cornflour

85g caster sugar

6 plain chocolate truffles (or use
  recipe on page 28)

strawberries, raspberries and
  blueberries, to decorate

FOR THE MINT FROTH:

150ml full-fat milk

1 tbsp crème de menthe

Pre-heat the oven to 180°C/350°F/Gas mark 4.

Finely grate 40g of the chocolate. Rub half the butter all over the inside of six tall dariole moulds (or similar containers). Dust well with the grated chocolate, shaking out any excess. Set aside on a baking tray.

Melt the remaining chocolate (including any shaken-out excess) and butter in a small heatproof bowl over a pan of barely simmering water, or in a microwave-proof bowl in the microwave on full power for 2–3 minutes, stirring once. Do not overheat or the chocolate will 'seize', or turn solid. Scrape this mixture into a bigger bowl, then beat in the ground almonds, egg yolks and cornflour.

Whisk the egg whites in a separate bowl until they form stiff but not dry peaks. Gradually beat in the caster sugar – you may prefer to use a hand-held electric whisk for this.

Fold the meringue mixture into the melted chocolate mixture. Spoon half the combined mixture into the base of the mould, place a chocolate truffle on top, then fill each mould with the remaining mixture. Smooth the tops of the fondants.

Bake the fondants in the oven for 10–15 minutes until risen and slightly wobbly (they're best eaten as soon as they're cooked).

Bring the milk to a boil, remove from the heat, add the crème de menthe, then 'froth' with a hand blender. Turn the fondants out onto plates and serve with fresh berries and mint froth.

Fig fritters

This is a great dessert for those of you who don't want the fuss of making something beforehand. I use figs grown in my garden and simply fry them in batter at the last minute. While the figs are in the deep-fat fryer, scoop your ice cream into bowls, add the drained fig fritters to the side and sprinkle with a little sugar.

SERVES 8

vegetable or sunflower oil, for
   deep-frying

8 large ripe figs

FOR THE FRITTER BATTER:

125g plain flour

125g rice flour

170g sugar

pinch of salt

1 egg

250ml ice-cold water

TO SERVE:

500ml ginger and syrup ice cream
   (see page 178)

50g julienned crystallized ginger

caster sugar, for sprinkling

Heat 7.5cm of oil in a deep, heavy pot to 180°C/350°F.

Wipe the figs with a damp cloth to remove any dust.

To make the batter, combine all the ingredients in a large bowl and whisk until just blended; don't worry if there are a few lumps.

Dip two figs into the batter and immediately deep-fry for about 2 minutes until golden brown. Using a wire-mesh skimmer or slotted metal spoon, carefully transfer to paper towels to drain. Repeat with the remaining figs.

To serve, put a small scoop of ginger and syrup ice cream in the centre of each bowl with a whole fig. Dust with caster sugar and sprinkle the crystallized ginger on the ice cream.

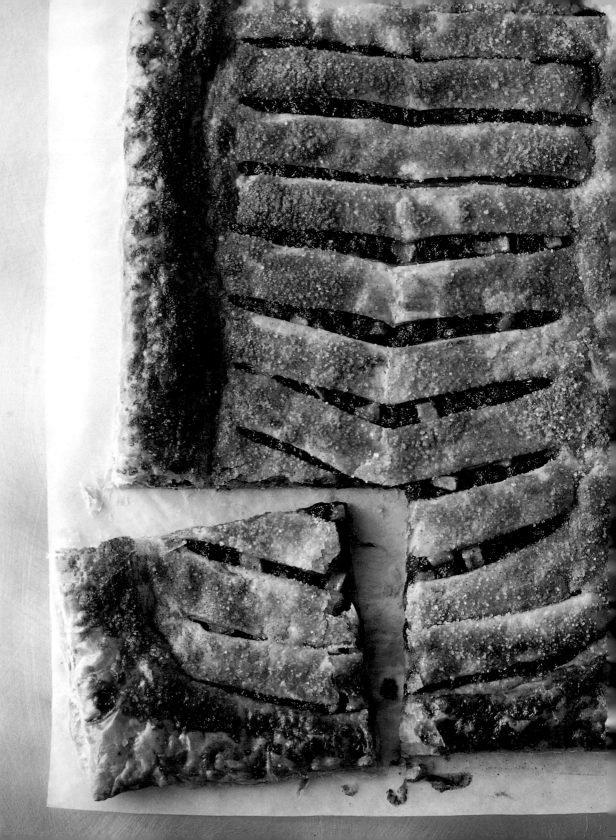

Mincemeat and apple jalousie
While thinking of ideas for this book, I flicked through one of my old college books and found a recipe for jalousie. I remember making at college and it worked well, so I tried this dish again 15 years later. It is still a real classic and deserves its place in this book.

SERVES 8

400g mincemeat

1 small Bramley cooking apple (225g), peeled, cored and finely chopped

zest of 1 orange

½ tsp ground mixed spice

2 tbsp rum

375g puff pastry (see page 15) or packet of fresh ready-rolled, all-butter puff pastry

plain flour, for dusting

1 large egg, lightly beaten

1 dsp golden granulated sugar, mixed with ¼ tsp ground cinnamon

caster sugar, for dusting

Pre-heat the oven to 200°C/400°F/Gas mark 6. Lightly grease a large, solid baking tray.

Place the mincemeat in a large bowl, then add the apple, orange zest, spice and rum and give it a good mix.

Unroll the pastry onto a surface lightly dusted with flour, and roll it into two slightly thinner rectangles, each measuring approximately 15 x 45cm.

Roll one of the pieces of pastry a little thinner and larger, then fold it in half lengthways. Using a sharp knife, cut diagonally about 5cm into the fold at 2.5cm intervals.

Place the second rectangle of pastry on the baking tray and pile the mincemeat filling onto the pastry, leaving a 2.5cm edge all around. Brush the edge with a little cold water.

Unfold the first rectangle of pastry and place it over the mincemeat. Using your thumbs, press the edges all around the filling to seal them. Finally, trim the pastry to 1cm around the filling and either crimp the edges with your fingers or use a knife.

Brush all over with the beaten egg, then sprinkle the sugar and cinnamon mixture over the top. Bake for 30–35 minutes and sprinkle with the icing sugar just before serving with cream or custard or, as my gran used to have it, with ice cream.

Roasted crab apples

I first stumbled upon crab apples while wandering round a market in London. I saw trays of these lovely small apples that people were ignoring and I couldn't understand why. When I tasted them, I discovered they have a very strong, sharp, bitter taste. While I was trying to invent a dish to go with Kentish pudding pie (see page 128), I thought these apples would be ideal, as their sharpness cuts through the sweetness of the dessert. Roasting them in sugar, plenty of butter and spices works very well. The secret with crab apples is you only need to roast them for about 5 minutes, otherwise they turn to purée.

SERVES 6

50g butter
500g crab apples
75g caster sugar
1 tsp ground cinnamon
2 cinnamon sticks, crumbled
icing sugar, for serving

Pre-heat the oven to 200°C/400°F/Gas mark 6.

Heat a frying pan until hot, then add the butter and heat until foaming. Add the crab apples and cook for 3–4 minutes until they are golden.

Tip the crab apples into a roasting tray and toss with the ground cinnamon and cinnamon sticks. Place in the oven for 4–6 minutes until just tender.

Serve with Kentish pudding pie (see page 128), junket ice cream (see page 182) and a dusting of icing sugar.

Slow-roasted peaches with orange caramel sauce

This is my version of the classic dish peach Melba which was created in the 1890s by the first true super-chef, Auguste Escoffier at London's Savoy Hotel. After hearing Nellie Melba, the Australian opera singer, perform at Covent Garden, he was inspired to create a dessert. The story is that she loved ice cream but it affected her voice. Escoffier produced a dessert with raspberries, sugar, ice cream and peaches, which he named peach Melba in her honour.

SERVES 6

250g caster sugar

250ml fresh orange juice

1 vanilla pod

100g pistachio nuts, shelled

75g whole almonds

6 medium white peaches

50g unsalted butter, softened until runny but not melted

150g fresh raspberries

almond ice cream (see page 176), for serving

Put 150g of the sugar in a heavy-based saucepan with 3 tbsp water and dissolve over a low heat. When the sugar syrup is completely clear, increase the heat and cook for about 5 minutes to a light caramel.

Remove from the heat and carefully stir in the orange juice (it will splutter). Slit open the vanilla pod, scrape out the seeds and add these to the caramel sauce. Set aside to cool until thickened, then stir in the pistachio nuts and whole almonds.

Pre-heat the oven to 170°C/340°F/Gas mark 3½.

Using a blowtorch, blacken the peach skins, then use a clean cloth to wipe the skins away.

Brush the peaches liberally with the butter using a pastry brush. Sprinkle them with the remaining sugar, making sure they are thoroughly coated (you can also place the sugar on a plate and roll the peaches in it).

Place the peaches in a small roasting tin and spoon the caramel over them. Roast, uncovered, in the oven for about 30 minutes until the peaches are softened but still whole, basting them with the pan juices every 10 minutes or so. Add the raspberries to the roasting tin for the final 10 minutes.

Remove from the oven, cover the tin loosely with foil and leave to cool – this encourages juices to gather in the bottom of the tin.

Serve the peaches with the orange caramel sauce spooned over and the almond ice cream on the side.

Cold puddings

Delice au cassis
This is an advanced pastry, but it is one of the best-looking and -tasting desserts in this book. To get a mirror finish on the glaze, quickly blowtorch the set jelly to make it flat and bubble-free.

SERVES 8–10

350g blackcurrants

150ml syrup, divided into 3 equal
  quantities (see below)

7½ gelatine leaves

12g powdered milk

½ vanilla pod

3 medium egg yolks

250g sugar

25cm ready-made sponge flan

200ml crème de cassis

1 quantity Italian meringue (made
  with 3 egg whites, 180g sugar,
  5 tbsp water – see page 35)

400ml double cream

blackcurrants, raspberries,
  strawberries, blackberries and
  a mint sprig, for decorating

FOR THE SYRUP:

375g sugar

325ml water

30g glucose

(Any leftover syrup can be
  stored in the fridge)

To make the syrup, place the ingredients in a pan and bring to the boil, stirring occasionally. Boil for about 3 minutes, skimming the surface if necessary. If using a saccharometer, the reading should be 30°C Beaumé or 1.2624 on the density scale. Pass the syrup through a conical strainer and leave until cold before using.

Purée the blackcurrants in the blender with 50ml syrup, then pass the purée through a conical strainer.

To make the mousse, soak 4½ gelatine leaves in cold water for 15 minutes, then drain. Reserve 4 tbsp blackcurrant purée and put the rest in a saucepan with the powdered milk and vanilla pod; bring to the boil. Whisk the yolks and sugar in a bowl until they form a ribbon. Pour the boiling purée onto the egg mixture, whisking continuously, then pour back into the pan over a low heat, stirring constantly with a spatula until the mousse coats the spatula. Do not boil. Remove from the heat and stir the drained gelatine into the mousse. Discard the vanilla, then strain the mousse into a bowl and leave to cool, stirring occasionally to prevent a skin forming.

Place the sponge flan on a serving plate. Mix together 50ml syrup and 1 tbsp purée and brush over the sponge. Place a 25cm flan ring, 6cm deep, onto the sponge and cut around to make the base.

When the mousse is lukewarm, gently fold in the meringue, then the crème de cassis, using a balloon whisk. Beat the double cream until it forms a ribbon. Using a spatula, gently fold into the mixture.

Now assemble the dessert immediately, before the mousse sets. Fill the flan ring with mousse, leaving a 3mm gap at the top. Smooth over the surface with a palette knife. Place in a freezer or very cold fridge for several hours.

To glaze, soak the remaining gelatine in cold water for 15 minutes, then drain well. Mix 50ml syrup with the remaining purée and stir in the drained gelatine. Pass through a muslin cloth into a jug, then glaze the top of the dessert. Leave to set in the fridge. To remove the ring, heat the outside of the ring with a blowtorch for a few seconds, then slide the ring up. Decorate with fruit to serve.

Puff pastry and raspberry stack

Rather than using an egg yolk or a mixture of egg and milk to glaze the puff pastry, dust it with icing sugar and cook in a really hot oven. This causes the pastry to rise and the icing sugar to caramelize, giving you a beautifully clear, smooth glaze.

SERVES 4

300g ready-rolled puff pastry

45g icing sugar, plus extra for dusting

400g fresh raspberries

75ml double cream

175g mascarpone cheese

50g fresh strawberries

sugar twists, optional (see pages 32–33)

Pre-heat the oven to 220°C/425°F/Gas mark 7.

Cut the puff pastry into circles with a diameter of 7.5cm. Place on a non-stick oven tray and leave to rest in the fridge for 10 minutes.

Turn the pastry over (this will ensure an even rise when baked) and dust with icing sugar. Bake in the top of the oven for 5–6 minutes. Remove from the oven and allow to cool, then carefully slice each pastry into three discs (top/middle/bottom).

To make the sauce, blend half the raspberries with 1 tbsp of the icing sugar and a little water and pass through a sieve.

Beat the cream, mascarpone and remaining sugar together.

Place a spoonful of the mascarpone mixture on top of one of the discs (the base disc) and top with a couple of halved strawberries. Place the raspberries around the edge, then top with another disc (the middle disc) of pastry and repeat the process. To finish, top with a final piece of pastry (the top disc).

Spoon the sauce onto a serving plate and place the puff pastry stack in the centre. Dust with icing sugar and serve with a sugar twist if you wish.

Ginger and syrup cheesecake

There are two ways of making a cheesecake – the oven-baked American style with a sponge base, and the English style which is a set mixture with a biscuit base. This is a quick version of the English style, using cream cheese mixed with ginger and syrup (the syrup adds the sugar to the mixture), simply placed on a biscuit base. It's a really easy cheesecake that works well if you are short of time.

SERVES 2

4 digestive biscuits

15g butter, softened

300g full-fat cream cheese

4 pieces of ginger in syrup, 2 diced

3 tbsp grated dark chocolate

2 sugar twists, optional (see pages 32–33)

Crush the biscuits and mix with the softened butter. Place two 5cm metal rings on serving plates and fill with the crumb mixture to form the base of the cheesecake.

Place the cream cheese in a bowl with the diced ginger and about 4 tbsp of the syrup and mix well. Spoon the mixture into the rings and level the top.

Top each cheesecake with the grated chocolate. Slice the remaining ginger in half and arrange on the top of the cheesecakes.

Place a warm cloth around the rings to loosen the cheesecakes, or briefly warm with a blowtorch, and carefully lift the rings off. Garnish with a sugar twist and serve.

Lemon curd syllabub

This is one of my favourite quick puddings – I don't know whether it's the fact that it can be made in minutes or the fact that it contains a small amount of white wine, enabling you to drink the rest of the bottle! The secret of this syllabub is that it must be made quite quickly and use good-quality lemon curd. Traditionally, a syllabub would be a mixture of egg yolks and sugar whisked over heat. My version uses cream as a base and it's far quicker. It should be served in the summertime following a light main course, such as poached salmon – the two flavours work well together.

SERVES 4

4 shortbread biscuits (or lemon-flavoured shortbread)

50ml white wine

75g mascarpone cheese

250ml double cream, plus extra for serving

4 tbsp icing sugar

8 tbsp lemon curd

2 tbsp flaked almonds, toasted

fresh mint sprigs

Crumble the shortbread into the bottom of four wine glasses and moisten with half the wine.

Mix the mascarpone and cream with the sugar. When it reaches soft peaks, fold in the remaining wine and swirl in the lemon curd, leaving a marbling of yellow through the cream.

Spoon the mixture into the glasses, top with a spoonful of double cream and scatter with the toasted almonds. Garnish with a sprig of mint and serve.

Limoncello with apricot and nut biscotti

I love Italy, and the biscotti in this recipe come from Tuscany and the limoncello from one of my favourite places, Capri, where the huge, juicy lemons have such an amazing flavour. Limoncello is traditionally a very alcoholic drink, containing some 90% alcohol, but if you make it this way with straight vodka you can sup it as an after-dinner drink. It must be served in really cold, iced shot glasses, straight out of the freezer. The Italian word 'biscotti' literally means 'twice baked'.

SERVES 6–8

FOR THE LIMONCELLO:

70cl fruit alcohol (40–80% proof) or vodka

200g caster sugar

zest and juice of 8 unwaxed lemons

FOR THE BISCOTTI:

250g plain flour

250g caster sugar

1½ tsp baking powder

3 medium eggs, lightly beaten

50g dried sweetened strawberries, chopped

100g dried apricots, chopped

50g medjool dates, pitted and chopped

75g shelled pistachio nuts

50g whole blanched almonds

50g shelled hazelnuts

zest of 1 lemon

To make the limoncello, warm a little of the vodka in a pan and add the sugar until it is all dissolved – don't let it boil. Remove from the heat when dissolved and add the lemon juice and zest. Add the remaining vodka, pour into a bottle and freeze.

To make the biscotti, pre-heat the oven to 180°C/350°F/Gas mark 4. Line a baking tray with baking parchment.

Mix the flour, sugar and baking powder in a large bowl. Add half the beaten eggs and mix well, then add half of what's left and mix again. Now add the last quarter a little bit at a time until the dough takes shape but isn't too wet (you may not need to use all of the eggs). Add the fruit, nuts and lemon zest and mix well.

Divide the dough into six, roll into sausage shapes about 3cm in diameter and place at least 6cm apart on the lined baking tray (wetting your hands before rolling these out helps to prevent the dough sticking). Lightly flatten the 'sausages'.

Bake for 20–30 minutes until golden brown. Remove from the oven and leave for 10 minutes to cool and firm up.

Using a serrated knife, cut the biscotti on an angle into slices 5mm thick (you should get about 30 slices). Lay the slices on the baking trays. Return to the oven and cook for 8 minutes, then turn the slices over and cook for a further 10–15 minutes or until a pale golden colour. Cool on wire racks, then store in airtight jars.

To serve, pour the limoncello into a shot glass (remove the zest before serving), with a couple of biscotti on the side.

Black Forest gâteau

This is the English name for a cake called Schwarzwälder which comes from southern Germany. It uses the two main ingredients from that region – kirsch and cherries. This is one of the desserts that is a real 1970s' classic – a bit like prawn cocktail – and I love them both.

SERVES 8–10

FOR THE SPONGE:

butter, for greasing

9 eggs

250g caster sugar

215g self-raising flour, sifted

40g cocoa powder

FOR THE FILLING AND TOPPING:

1 x 340g (drained weight) jar cherries

2 tbsp arrowroot

a good dash of Kirsch

750ml double cream, whipped

50g flaked almonds, toasted

FOR THE CHOCOLATE SHARDS:

300g dark chocolate

½ tsp peppermint essence

110g demerara sugar

Pre-heat the oven to 180°C/350°F/Gas mark 4. Grease and line a deep 26cm springform cake tin.

Break the eggs into a mixing bowl, add the sugar and whisk well until the ribbon stage, or very light and fluffy. Carefully fold in the sifted flour and cocoa powder.

Pour the mix into the prepared tin and bake for about 55 minutes or until cooked. Turn out onto a wire rack and leave to cool.

Drain the cherries, reserving the juice. Put the juice into a pan and bring to the boil. While the juice is heating, mix the arrowroot with a little water in a small bowl, to slacken to a paste. When the cherry juice is boiling, mix the arrowroot paste into it. Strain through a sieve over the cherries with the Kirsch and leave to one side to cool.

Slice the sponge into three layers using a sharp knife. Sandwich the three layers together using the whipped cream and half the cherries and almonds.

Melt the chocolate in a bowl over a pan of simmering water. Add the peppermint essence and sugar, stir and spread onto a tray lined with clingfilm. Place in the fridge to set.

When the chocolate is set, break it into large shards and stick randomly around the edge of the cake (if necessary, place a blob of cream on the back of the shards to help them stay in place).

Top with the remaining cherries and serve.

Quick strawberry and vanilla gâteau

This recipe saves time by using a sponge flan case, although you wouldn't know by looking at it. The trick is to flavour the creamy filling – I use bought, ready-made custard as this creates a better-tasting filling.

SERVES 6–8

1 large ready-made flan case

750ml double cream

100g caster sugar

1 vanilla pod, seeds only

1 shot of Drambuie

200ml ready-made custard

1 punnet of small strawberries

1½ punnets of large strawberries

1 punnet of mixed berries, such as redcurrants, blueberries and blackberries

50g icing sugar

fresh mint sprigs

Using a 20–25cm stainless steel ring, cut out the centre of the flan. With a sharp knife, slice the disc in half through the middle so you end up with two thin discs.

Whip the double cream with 25g of the caster sugar, the vanilla seeds and a shot of Drambuie to a thick peak consistency. Fold in the custard, then chill in the fridge.

Set aside 10 whole, small strawberries for the garnish. Cut the green top from all the remaining strawberries and cut them in half lengthways.

Place one sponge disk in the bottom of the ring then line the ring with the largest strawberry halves, cut side against the ring. You won't need all of the strawberries so save the remainder for the topping. Place the whipped cream in the ring and gently spread to the edges. Add the rest of the strawberries and smooth the top.

Place the remaining disc of sponge on top and lift the cake onto a plate and remove the ring by carefully warming the edges with a hot cloth and lifting it straight off.

Place the remaining caster sugar into a very clean pan and heat gently until it caramelizes, then remove from the heat and leave to cool slightly.

While this is cooling, take a metal skewer that has been heated until red hot and score the top of the gâteau in lines to create a diamond pattern. Once cooled, the caramelised sugar should be made into spun sugar (see page 32) and placed on top of the dish. Dress the top with the remaining strawberries and the berries. Sprinkle over the sieved icing sugar and garnish with sprigs of fresh mint.

Baked chocolate mousse with candied fennel root

Do try this recipe as I think it's one of the best in the book. This is for all the requests I get for a gluten-free cake. It's fab with fennel or ground nutmeg or just leave it plain, but it must be eaten at room temperature and never put in the fridge as it firms up too much. It will rise and then fall after coming out of the oven, but don't worry.

SERVES 6–8

½ fennel bulb, thinly sliced

300g dark bitter chocolate (minimum 60% cocoa fat)

150g unsalted butter

6 eggs, separated

50g caster sugar

150ml whipped double cream, to serve

FOR THE CANDIED FENNEL:

1 fennel bulb

100g caster sugar

100ml water

Pre-heat the oven to 180°C/350°F/Gas mark 4. Line the base and sides of a 20cm spring-bottomed cake tin with greaseproof paper and add the slices of fennel on to the base.

Melt the chocolate and butter in a metal bowl placed over a pan of simmering water.

Whisk the egg yolks with 2 tbsp of the sugar for 30 seconds. Stir in the melted chocolate and mix well.

Beat the egg whites with the remaining sugar until very stiff, then quickly fold one-third of the whites into the chocolate mix. Gently fold in the remainder and pour the mix into the cake tin.

Place on the middle shelf of the oven and bake for 20 minutes. Remove from the oven and allow to cool before serving.

To make the candied fennel root, slice the fennel bulb and add to a pan with the sugar and 100ml water. Bring to the boil and simmer for 20–30 minutes and allow to cool.

Serve in a wedge with some of the fennel and juices and a spoonful of whipped cream.

Profiteroles

I think of this dessert as comfort food for grown-ups. Try not to make the sauce too thick as it can spoil the whole dish – that's why I like to make it with sugar stock rather than double cream.

SERVES 4–6

FOR THE CHOUX PASTRY:

85g unsalted butter

4 tsp caster sugar

115g plain flour

pinch of salt

3 medium eggs, beaten

FOR THE CREAM FILLING:

600ml double cream

zest of 3 oranges

FOR THE CHOCOLATE SAUCE:

50g caster sugar

175g good-quality plain chocolate, broken into pieces

Pre-heat the oven to 200°C/400°F/Gas mark 6. Lightly oil a large baking tray.

To make the pastry, place the butter and sugar into a large pan with 200ml cold water. Place over a low heat to melt the butter, then increase the heat and shoot in the flour and salt all at once.

Remove from the heat and quickly beat the mixture vigorously until a smooth paste is formed. When the mixture is smooth, replace the pan over the heat and stir with the spatula for 1 minute. Immediately add the eggs, off the heat, one at a time, mixing in with a spatula. Continue beating until the paste is smooth and glossy; you should have a soft dropping consistency. The mixture will be shiny and smooth and fall from a spoon if given a sharp tap.

Dip a teaspoon into some warm water and lift out a spoon of the profiterole mixture. Rub the top of the mixture with a wet finger to get rid of any bumps and spoon onto the baking tray.

Place in the oven and before closing the door, throw in half a cup of water into the bottom of the oven and shut the door quickly. This will make more steam in the oven and make the choux pastry rise better. Bake for 10–20 minutes, until golden brown (if too pale they will become soggy when cool).

Remove from the oven and prick the base of each profiterole. Place on the baking tray with the hole facing upwards and return to the oven for 5 minutes where the warm air helps to dry out the centres.

To make the filling, lightly whip the cream with the zest until soft peaks form. Do not over-whip. When the profiteroles are cold, using a piping bag with a plain 5mm nozzle, pipe the cream into the holes of the profiteroles.

To make the chocolate sauce, melt the chocolate in a bowl over a pan of simmering water. Put the sugar in a small pan with 100ml water and bring to the boil. Stir the melted chocolate, then add the water and sugar mixture and stir until smooth and shiny. Arrange the buns on a serving dish and pour over the hot sauce. Eat hot or cold.

Figs in vanilla syrup

These delicious figs make great gifts when placed in an attractive glass jar. They are best served with a big dollop of vanilla or white chocolate ice cream (see pages 176 and 177).

MAKES 500G

8–9 firm fresh figs, halved

100g caster sugar

½ vanilla pod, split lengthways

½ cinnamon stick

½ tsp citric acid

Pre-heat the oven to 150°C/300°F/Gas mark 2.

Place the figs in a warmed ovenproof jar with the cut sides facing outwards. Pack the centre of the jar tightly with figs and put two halves cut-side uppermost in the top of the jar.

Put the sugar, vanilla pod and cinnamon stick into a saucepan with 400ml water. Slowly bring to the boil and heat stirring continuously until the sugar has completely dissolved. Boil for 1 minute, then remove from the heat.

Lift the vanilla pod out of the syrup. Using a small knife, scrape the black seeds into the syrup and stir in the citric acid. Remove the cinnamon stick. Tuck the vanilla pod down the side of the jar.

Pour the syrup over the figs to cover completely and come almost to the brim of the jar. Cover the top of the jar with a piece of foil. Stand the jar on a baking tray lined with several sheets of folded newspaper and bake in the pre-heated oven for 20–30 minutes until the syrup has turned a delicate pink and the figs are just beginning to rise in the jar.

Using oven gloves or a cloth, transfer the jar to a wooden board, close the clasp fully and leave to cool completely. When cold, check the jar is properly sealed. Label and store in a cool, dark place. The figs will keep for 6–12 months.

Petits Monts Blancs

This is a great recipe which deserves to be more popular. I think the last time I had this dessert was in a pâtisserie in Paris and it was fab (and to be honest, I had another portion straight away). If you can't find crème de marrons de l'Ardeche (sweetened chestnut purée), simply beat approximately 200g chestnut purée with 125g icing sugar until smooth.

SERVES 8

FOR THE MERINGUE:

2 large egg whites

110g white caster sugar

FOR THE FILLING:

2 x 250g tins crème de marrons
de l'Ardeche, chilled

FOR THE MASCARPONE CREAM:

250g mascarpone cheese

200ml fromage frais

1 rounded dsp caster sugar

1 tsp pure vanilla extract

a little icing sugar, for dusting

Preheat the oven to 150°C/300°F/Gas mark 2. Line a baking tray with baking parchment or a non-stick cooking mat.

To make the meringue, place the egg whites in a large clean bowl and, using an electric whisk on a low speed, begin whisking. Continue for about 2 minutes until the whites are foamy, then switch the speed to medium and carry on whisking until the egg whites reach the stiff peak stage. Next, whisk the sugar in on high, a dessertspoon at a time, until you have a stiff and glossy mixture.

Spoon 8 heaped dessertspoons of the mixture onto the baking tray, spacing them evenly. Using the back of the spoon or a small palette knife, hollow out the centres.

Place on the centre shelf of the oven, immediately reduce the heat to 140°C/275°F/Gas mark 1 and leave them for 30 minutes. After that, turn the oven off and leave the meringues to dry out in the warmth of the oven until it is completely cold (usually about 4 hours or overnight). The meringues will store well in a tin or plastic box, and will even freeze extremely well.

To assemble the Monts Blancs, spoon equal quantities of the crème de marrons into each meringue.

Whisk all the ingredients (except the icing sugar) for the mascarpone cream together, then spoon equal amounts on top of the chestnut purée. A light dusting of icing sugar helps them resemble the snowcapped mountain they are named after.

Baked chocolate and orange cheesecake

This is a classic American way of making a cheesecake (the British version usually has a biscuit base and is set, whereas this has sponge and is baked). Cheesecakes are one of the oldest recorded desserts and they are said to have been served at the first Olympic games in 776BC, though I bet they didn't taste like this.

SERVES 8–10

butter, for greasing

23cm sponge (cut from a large bought flan case)

3 tbsp Grand Marnier

200g caster sugar

zest of 2 oranges

juice of 1 orange

4 level tbsp cornflour

850g full-fat soft cream cheese

3 medium eggs

1 vanilla pod

375ml double cream, plus extra for serving

36 dark chocolate pieces

FOR THE MARBLED CHOCOLATE:

150g white chocolate

150g dark chocolate

Pre-heat the oven to 180°C/350°F/Gas mark 4. Butter a 23cm springform cake tin.

Cut the sponge horizontally into two discs. Use one to line the cake tin. Drizzle with 1 tbsp Grand Marnier.

Mix together the sugar, orange zest and juice and cornflour in a bowl using a wooden spoon, then use an electric hand mixer to beat in the cream cheese. Add the eggs one by one, beating constantly until all the eggs are well incorporated.

Slice open the vanilla pod, remove the seeds with a sharp knife and place the seeds into the cream mixture, add 2 tbsp of Grand Marnier, if using, and mix everything together well. Add the cream and beat well until the mixture is smooth.

Pour half of the mixture gently over the sponge base in the cake tin. Top with half of the chocolate pieces and smooth over with a stepped palette knife. Repeat once more.

Sit the tin in a baking tray filled with 2–3mm of warm water to help create steam during cooking. Place in the oven and bake for 50 minutes until the top is golden. Remove from the oven and leave to cool and set completely before removing from the tin.

Meanwhile, melt the white and dark chocolate separately in bowls over simmering water. Cover a baking tray tightly in cling film. Pour the dark chocolate and the white chocolate onto the tray. Using your finger, swirl the two chocolates together to create a marble effect. Chill to set.

Serve the cheesecake cut into wedges, with a piece of the marbled chocolate and a drizzle of cream.

Crème caramel

A lot of people think that this dessert should be served on its own, but for me it's best served with fresh berries or oranges. It is also known as a flan or caramel custard in some countries.

SERVES 6

150ml milk
275ml double cream
4 large eggs
40g caster sugar
1 vanilla pod, seeds only

FOR THE CARAMEL:
110g caster sugar

Pre-heat the oven to 140°C/275°F/Gas mark 1.

First, make the caramel. Put the 110g sugar in a saucepan over a high heat. When the sugar begins to melt, cook until it has become a uniform liquid syrup about two or three shades darker than golden syrup.

Take the pan off the heat and carefully add 2 tbsp of hot tap water – it will splutter and bubble a bit but will soon stop. Stir and when the syrup is smooth once again, quickly pour it into the base of six ramekins, tipping them around to coat the sides a little.

Pour the milk and cream into another pan and leave it to heat gently while you whisk together the eggs, sugar and vanilla seeds in a large bowl. When the milk and cream are steaming hot, pour onto the egg and sugar mixture, whisking thoroughly until blended. Pour the liquid into the ramekins.

Place the ramekins in a large roasting tray. Transfer the tray carefully to the oven, then pour hot water into it to come two-thirds of the way up the sides of the ramekins. Bake for 45–60 minutes.

Cool and chill the crème caramel. Remove from the fridge 1 hour before you are ready to serve them. Free the edges by running a knife around before inverting them onto serving plates.

Raspberry and nougat semifreddo

I first stumbled across semifreddo in Italy where I tried it with nougat inside. Semifreddo in Italian translates to 'half cold'. The Spanish also have a dessert very similar called semifrio. This is a standard recipe which you can vary, for instance using strawberries instead of raspberries. You can omit the nougat if you wish, and the recipe works well with pistachios and hazelnuts and also fruit such as lemon – lemon and vodka semifreddo with hazelnuts is fantastic.

SERVES 8

olive oil, for greasing

400g mascarpone cheese

4 eggs

6 tbsp caster sugar

200g raspberries

100g nougat with pistachio nuts, chopped

TO SERVE:

fresh raspberries

8 fresh doughnuts

raspberry sauce (see page 43)

Grease a small loaf tin with olive oil, then line with clingfilm.

Separate the egg yolks and the whites into two bowls.

Add the sugar to the egg yolks and whisk until frothy. Add the mascarpone and keep mixing, then fold in the chopped nougat.

Whip up the egg whites, then carefully fold them into the mixed yolks with the raspberries.

Pour the mixture into the lined tin and freeze until set (preferably overnight).

To serve, tip the semifreddo out of the mould onto a serving plate. Serve a slice of the semifreddo with some raspberries and a doughnut and with a little raspberry sauce drizzled over the top.

Vanilla panna cotta with balsamic berries

Panna cotta simply translates as 'cooked cream'. However, this recipe is very light and delicate due to the gelatine. You must be careful with the amount of gelatine you put in – just enough to hold it firm; use too much and you will end up with a dessert you can bounce off the walls. The addition of balsamic berries adds a lovely sharpness which goes well with the creaminess of the panna cotta.

SERVES 6–8

4 leaves of gelatine

120ml milk

zest of 2 oranges

2 vanilla pods, split

150g caster sugar

1.2 litres double cream

80ml vodka

FOR THE BALSAMIC BERRIES:

200g strawberries, hulled

150g raspberries

100g blueberries

75ml good-quality aged balsamic vinegar

25g caster sugar

Soak the gelatine in the milk and leave to one side.

Place the orange zest, vanilla pods and caster sugar in a pan. Add 800ml of the cream and bring to the boil. Simmer until the mixture is reduced by a third.

While the cream is reducing, remove the gelatine from the milk and place the milk in a pan to warm gently. When it is warm, add the soaked gelatine and stir to dissolve. Add to the warm cream and pass through a sieve and leave to cool.

Lightly whip the remaining cream and fold into the setting mixture, together with the vodka. Pour the mixture into 6–8 dariole moulds, ramekins or similar sized moulds and place in the fridge to set.

While the panna cotta is setting, make the balsamic berries. Place the strawberries, raspberries, blueberries, balsamic vinegar and sugar into a large bowl and toss together. Allow to marinate for 2–3 hours, tossing occasionally.

Remove the panna cotta from the fridge and slide a knife around the edge to loosen. Alternatively, dip the moulds very briefly in hot water to loosen the panna cotta. Tip them out into the middle of the plates and spoon the balsamic berries around the edge.

Jellied raspberry and vodka terrine with lime syrup

This is a grown-up version of kids' raspberry jelly! The vodka adds a good flavour to the raspberry terrine and the lime syrup adds a lovely kick. The secret is to use arrowroot as this will keep the sauce clear; if you use cornflour to thicken it, it will create a cloudy sauce. I love serving this dish whole as it looks so impressive. You can mix and match the fruit with this recipe – try layers of mango raspberries, strawberries and blueberries. Pineapple is the only fruit which doesn't work well as it contains an acid which causes the jelly to dissolve, giving you a soup rather than a terrine.

SERVES 10

450g caster sugar
8 gelatine leaves
olive oil, for greasing
70–100ml vodka, to taste
3 x 225g punnets of raspberries

FOR THE SAUCE:
150g caster sugar
zest and juice of 5 limes
1 tsp arrowroot

Make the jelly by bringing the sugar and 1 litre of water to the boil. Meanwhile, soak the gelatine in some cold water. When the water has boiled, add the squeezed-out gelatine to the pan and mix gently. Pass through a sieve into a bowl and allow to cool until it is just starting to thicken.

Line a terrine mould first with olive oil and then with clingfilm. Pour the vodka into the setting syrup. Spoon a little of the jelly into the base of the terrine and allow it to start to set. Layer the raspberries with a little of the jelly to set each layer. Allow to set.

To make the sauce, place the sugar and lime juice in a pan with 150ml water and bring to a simmer. Dissolve the arrowroot in a little water and, using a whisk, mix it into the pan little by little until you have a sauce consistency. Pass through a sieve and add the zest and allow to cool.

Turn the terrine out of the mould onto a serving plate and remove the clingfilm. Serve the sauce separately.

Clotted cream summer pudding

Summer pudding brings back both good and bad memories of my childhood cooking – the good memory is of the taste and the bad one of cleaning the bottom of the fridge after it had leaked everywhere. Thankfully this recipe, made in individual moulds, solves that problem.

SERVES 4

400g mixed frozen fruits, defrosted

50g icing sugar, plus extra for dusting

10 slices white bread

1 small tub clotted cream

1 punnet each of strawberries, blueberries, raspberries and redcurrants

Place half the frozen fruit in a blender and whiz to purée the fruit well. Add some sugar to taste.

Line four small moulds or small pudding basins with clingfilm. Remove the crusts from the bread and cut circles to fit the base of the moulds. Dip one side of the bread circles into the puréed fruit and use to line the base of the basin, dipped side facing out. Line the sides of the moulds with more dipped bread, dipped-side out.

Half-fill the centre of each mould with some of the defrosted fruit, then add a teaspoon of clotted cream. Top with the remaining defrosted fruit and some of the juices, then top with another circle of dipped bread.

Chill the puddings in the fridge for at least 30 minutes before serving.

To serve, tip the puddings out from the moulds onto serving plates. Pour over the remaining puréed sauce, scatter the fruit around the pudding and dust with icing sugar.

Strawberry jelly

Everyone loves jelly – I used to eat it raw, whereas my mother would cube it into a bowl, pour boiling water over, then tip it in a rabbit mould. But times move on and this is my homemade one, without the rabbit mould.

SERVES 4–6

600g strawberries, hulled

100g caster sugar

juice of 1 lemon

8 sheets of leaf gelatine

2 tbsp crème de peche

double cream and whipped cream, to serve

Slice 500g of the strawberries and place in a large heatproof bowl set over a pan of gently simmering water. Stir in the sugar and lemon juice.

Cover the bowl with clingfilm and leave for 30–40 minutes, checking the water in the pan occasionally and topping up with boiling water as necessary. The fruits will yield a clear, pink, fragrant juice.

Meanwhile, line a large sieve with wet muslin and place over a clean bowl. Pour the strawberry jus into the sieve and leave it to drip through, but don't rub the pulp otherwise the jus will lose its clarity. Discard the fruit pulp.

Soften the gelatine sheets in cold water. Meanwhile, pour the strawberry jus into a clean pan and heat until on the point of boiling, then take off the heat. Remove the gelatine from the cold water, squeezing out any excess water and then slip the gelatine into the hot jus, whisking until dissolved. Pass through a sieve into a bowl.

Allow to cool, then mix in 75ml water and the crème de peche. Leave until the jelly is cold and just on the point of setting. Meanwhile, place 4–6 wine glasses in the fridge and allow to chill.

Slice the remaining strawberries. Dip the strawberry slices quickly into a little of the setting jelly and stick to the inside of the chilled wine glasses.

Now for the fun bit. To make this jelly sparkle, whisk the setting jelly until lightly frothy and divide it among the glasses. Chill until completely set.

To serve, top with a thin float of double cream and a spoonful of whipped cream – keep it simple.

Raspberry and passion fruit Pavlova

Hailing from Australia, this classic dessert is named after the Russian ballerina Anna Pavlova. If you prefer a sticky meringue, add the cornflour and white wine vinegar listed in the ingredients as these will give you that wonderfully gooey texture.

SERVES 4–6

1 quantity cold meringue (see page 34)

2 tsp cornflour

1 tsp white wine vinegar

250ml double cream

5 passion fruit

150g white chocolate, melted

500g fresh raspberries

mint sprigs

Pre-heat the oven to 140°C/275°F/Gas mark 1. Cover a large baking tray with non-stick baking parchment.

Take the made-up meringue and fold in the cornflour and vinegar. Spoon the mixture onto the baking tray and spread into a large nest shape (or 10 small ones).

Place in the oven and cook for 10 minutes, then turn the heat down to its lowest setting for a few hours or leave overnight.

To serve, whip the cream into soft peaks. Cut open the passion fruit and spoon the insides into a bowl. Brush the melted white chocolate into the centre of the meringue and fill with the whipped cream.

Sprinkle over the fresh raspberries, then spoon over the passion fruit pulp. Top with fresh sprigs of mint and serve.

Raspberry marshmallows

Once you make marshmallows for the first time, you will never buy them again. Having said that, I remember going to the corner shop with my 50p pocket money and buying a quarter of flumps and a pack of candy cigarettes. If you want to keep these for longer in a jar, don't put fresh fruit inside – just leave them plain. If you wish to colour the marshmallow, add a few drops of food colouring to the mixture. These are also good dipped into a fondue of melted white chocolate.

MAKES ABOUT 450G

455g granulated sugar

1 tbsp liquid glucose

9 sheets of gelatine

2 large egg whites

1 tsp vanilla extract

oil, for greasing

125g fresh raspberries, coated in icing sugar or cornflour

icing sugar, for dusting

cornflour, for dusting

Put the granulated sugar, glucose and 200ml water in a heavy-based saucepan. Bring to the boil and continue cooking until it reaches 127°C/260°F on a sugar thermometer.

Meanwhile, soak the gelatine in 140ml cold water. Beat the egg whites until stiff. When the syrup is up to temperature, carefully slide in the softened gelatine sheets and their soaking water. The syrup will bubble up, so take care not to burn yourself. Pour the syrup into a metal jug.

Continue to beat the egg whites (preferably with an electric whisk) while pouring in the hot syrup from the jug. The mixture will become shiny and start to thicken. Add the vanilla extract and continue whisking for about 5–10 minutes, until the mixture is stiff and thick enough to hold its shape on the whisk.

Lightly oil a shallow 30 x 20cm baking tray. Dust it with sieved icing sugar and cornflour, then spoon half the mixture over and smooth it with a wet palette knife if necessary.

Roughly break the raspberries in half and spread over the marshmallow, then top with the remaining marshmallow. Leave to set in the fridge for at least 1 hour.

Dust the work surface with more icing sugar and cornflour. Loosen the marshmallow around the sides of the tray with a palette knife, then turn it out onto the dusted surface. Cut into squares and roll in the sugar and cornflour. Leave to dry a little on a wire rack, then pack into an airtight box.

Membrello

This recipe is also known as quince cheese. Quince, like apples, produce a natural pectin, making them ideal for jellying, and this Spanish recipe is a set jelly. The fruit originally comes from Turkey and Iran and is almost a cross between a pear and an apple, rather like like a fat pear. Peeled and then mixed to create this fantastic jelly, it tastes superb. Serve on its own, in an apple tart, apple pie or with some cheese such as Stilton.

SERVES 12–14

1kg preserving sugar
1kg quince, peeled, cored and
    grated

Place the sugar and 700ml water in a saucepan set over a gentle heat. Add the grated quince and bring to a boil, then turn down to a simmer and cook, uncovered, for 2 hours, stirring occasionally until the liquid has thickened and comes away from the sides of the pan when stirred.

Remove from the heat, allow to cool slightly, then pour into a tin or mould lined with clingfilm.

Refrigerate for at least 2 hours before unwrapping and serving with cheese and biscuits. Membrello will keep for a few months.

Tarts and flans

Apple and thyme tarte tatin

Would you believe it? There is actually a website called www.tarte-tatin.com. Only the French would have a website giving the history of this pudding. It was invented by the two Tatin sisters, Stephanie and Caroline. Stephanie was a particularly fine cook but not the brightest of people, her speciality being an apple tart served with a perfectly caramelized crust which melted in the mouth. One day Stephanie placed her tart the wrong way in the oven, with the pastry and the apples upside down. Nevertheless, the tart was served and one of the most famous desserts of all was created.

SERVES 4–6

150g caster sugar

25g butter

375g puff pastry (see page 15) or packet of fresh, ready-rolled all-butter puff pastry

flour, for rolling out

6 Golden Delicious apples, peeled, cored and cut into quarters

leaves from 2 thyme sprigs

Pre-heat the oven to 200°C/400°F/Gas mark 6.

To make the caramel, put the sugar into a 20cm ovenproof pan and heat gently without stirring until it turns golden brown. Remove from the heat, add the butter and stir in gently.

Roll out the puff pastry on a lightly floured surface. Cut out a circle slightly larger than the pan.

Place the apples peeled-side down into the pan and sprinkle with the fresh thyme leaves. Cover the apples and caramel mixture with the pastry and tuck the overlapped edges down the side of the pan.

Bake in the oven for 20–25 minutes until the pastry is brown.

Remove the pan from the oven and leave to rest for 1 minute before turning it out. To do this, place a plate on top of the pan, and invert so that the tart slips out, pastry to the base, apples on the top. Serve hot with ice cream on the side.

Fruit mille-feuille

This translates as 'dessert of a thousand layers'. It must be made with puff pastry, not filo which I've occasionally come across. Make sure you cook the puff pastry right through, as undercooked puff pastry tastes really horrible.

SERVES 8

225g puff pastry (see page 15) or packet of fresh, ready-rolled all-butter puff pastry

flour, for rolling out

1 egg, beaten

150ml double cream

1 dsp icing sugar, sifted, plus extra for dusting

1 vanilla pod, split

75ml ready-made custard

300g raspberries

250g strawberries, hulled and cut in half

1 fig, chopped

100g blueberries

Pre-heat the oven to 180°C/350°F/Gas mark 4.

Roll the pastry on a lightly floured surface and cut out a rectangle measuring 12.5 x 31cm. Place on a non-stick baking tray and brush the top with the egg wash.

Bake in the oven for 15–20 minutes, until well risen and golden brown. Remove from the oven, transfer to a wire rack and allow to cool.

Meanwhile, whip the cream, sugar and vanilla seeds to form soft peaks. Fold in the custard to combine.

Once the pastry is cool, cut it in half horizontally and then spread the base with two-thirds of the cream mixture.

Toss all the prepared fruit together in a bowl, and sprinkle the fruit over the cream. Spread the remaining cream mixture over the bottom of the top side of pastry and then sandwich together. Dust generously with icing sugar to serve.

Classic lemon tart

For me, this is a true chef's pudding. Pastry chefs would always choose this from a restaurant menu as it sorts the men from the boys. It shows how far you dare go in getting the filling thick and the pastry thin, because if the tart splits during baking, you'll spend all day cleaning the oven! Use plenty of icing sugar on the glaze.

SERVES 8

7 eggs

280g caster sugar

350ml double cream

zest and juice of 6 lemons

butter, for greasing

225g sweet shortcrust pastry (see page 14)

TO SERVE:

100g mild goat's cheese

50ml double cream

2 tbsp icing sugar, plus extra for dusting

a little whipped cream

Pre-heat the oven to 200°C/400°F/Gas mark 6.

To make the filling, break the eggs into a bowl and whisk gently to break up the yolks. Add the sugar and continue to mix, then add the cream and the lemon juice, but not the zest. Pass the mixture through a sieve, add the lemon zest and leave to one side.

Butter a 20cm plain, loose bottomed flan tin with softened butter and roll out the pastry between two wooden rulers (if you have some) to get a thin but even depth to the pastry. Carefully roll the pastry back onto the rolling pin, lift over the tin and roll the pastry back over the tin very loosely. If you don't leave plenty of slack, the pastry will rip or shrink too much when cooking. Tuck the pastry down the sides of the tin, pressing into the bottom edge well, but be careful not to tear or stretch the pastry. Don't trim the pastry.

Line the tart with a circle of greaseproof paper that is bigger than the tart and allows the paper to rise above the ring. Fill the tart with either baking beans, rice or ceramic baking beans. Bake for about 10 minutes.

Remove from the oven and remove the beans and greaseproof paper, then place back in the oven to colour the bottom of the tart. This should only take 3–4 minutes.

Turn the oven down to 100°C/225°F/Gas mark ½. Pour in the lemon mix to reach the top of the tart and bake for about 1 hour until the tart is only just set. Remove from the oven and trim off the edges of the pastry. Leave to cool for about 1 hour.

To make the accompanying cream, mix the goat's cheese with the double cream and icing sugar.

To serve, dust the tart with plenty of icing sugar and grill under a hot grill to caramelize the top. Remove from the grill and cut into wedges and serve with a spoonful of the cream.

French fruit tart

As a teenage student, I spent four months on work experience in a bakery in France. This was one of the dishes I learnt. It's so simple – just great pastry, fresh cream and fresh fruit. What could be easier?

SERVES 10

350g puff pastry (see page 15) or packet of fresh, ready-rolled all-butter puff pastry

plain flour, for rolling out

1 egg, beaten

85g white chocolate, broken into pieces

½ a vanilla pod, seeds only

200ml double cream, half whipped

100ml fresh custard (see page 44)

small punnet of medium-sized strawberries, hulled and halved

small punnet of blackberries and raspberries

1 large banana, sliced

small bunch of seedless green and/or black grapes, halved

4 tbsp smooth apricot jam

On a lightly floured surface, roll out the pastry and cut out a rectangle measuring 36 x 20cm. Place on a baking tray. Using a table knife, score a 1cm border around the edge, making sure you don't cut the pastry all the way through. Hold the knife like a pen, place your index finger against the outer edge of the pastry and run the knife along.

Brush the border with egg wash, taking care not to allow any to dribble down the sides because this will prevent the pastry rising evenly. Prick the base of the tart (not the border) with a fork and chill the pastry for 20 minutes.

Pre-heat the oven to 200°C/400°F/Gas mark 6.

Bake the pastry for 20–25 minutes until golden brown and crisp. Slide onto a wire rack and leave to cool. Once cooled, gently press the centre of the pastry down to leave the frame around the edge.

Melt the chocolate and brush over the bottom of the pastry. Leave to set.

Add the vanilla seeds to the cream and fold in the custard. Spoon and spread the cream mixture over the pastry base. Draw shallow lines in the cream mixture to create five sections and arrange the fruit on top so that each section is a contrasting colour.

Heat the jam and, using a pastry brush, glaze the fruit. Allow to set before serving.

Truffle torte

Traditionally, a torte is a kind of tart made with a dough of nuts (usually almonds), with a criss-cross pattern on the top with the pastry. I have just given this recipe the title as I think it sounds so much nicer than chocolate tart.

SERVES 10

butter, for greasing

110g amaretti biscuits

450g dark chocolate (70–75% cocoa solids)

4 tbsp liquid glucose

4 tbsp rum

650ml double cream, at room temperature

TO SERVE:

cocoa powder, for dusting

single cream, chilled

Line a 23cm cake tin with baking parchment and grease the base and sides with soft butter.

Crush the biscuits and place over the base of the tin.

Break the chocolate into squares and put them in a heatproof bowl, with the liquid glucose and rum. Place the bowl over a pan of barely simmering water, making sure the base of the bowl doesn't touch the water, then leave it until the chocolate has melted and become quite smooth. Stir, then take off the heat and leave the mixture to cool slightly.

In a separate bowl beat the double cream until only very slightly thickened. Fold half into the chocolate mixture, then fold that mixture into the rest of the cream. When it is smoothly blended, spoon it into the prepared tin. Tap the tin gently to even the mixture out, cover with clingfilm and chill overnight.

Just before serving, run a warm knife round the edge to loosen the torte, then remove from the mould.

To serve, dust the surface with sifted cocoa powder and serve with single cream.

Prune and almond tart

This is a real classic and must always be served warm or at room temperature. If you don't have time to make ice cream, serve this with pouring cream or, even better, thick clotted cream. Any unused frangipane can be stored in the fridge for a few days.

SERVES 4

FOR THE FRANGIPANE:

225g unsalted butter

225g caster sugar

175g ground almonds

50g plain flour

4 eggs

4 tbsp brandy

FOR THE TARTS:

200g shortcrust pastry (see page 14)

2 tbsp raspberry jam

275g frangipane (see above)

225g soft pitted prunes

10g flaked almonds

vanilla ice cream (see page 176), to serve

Make the pastry as on page 14. Pre-heat the oven to 180°C/350°F/ Gas mark 4. Lightly grease four 10cm fluted, round, loose-bottomed moulds, about 2.5cm deep.

To make the frangipane, cream the butter and sugar together until almost white. Mix together the ground almonds and flour in a separate bowl. Add one egg at a time to the butter and sugar mixture, sprinkling in a handful of the almond and flour at the same time (this helps the butter and sugar cream to mix in the eggs). Once all the eggs have been added, drizzle with the brandy, continue to mix in the remaining almond and flour.

Roll out the pastry and line the tart cases. Spread the jam on the base of the tarts, then fill with the frangipane. Finish by sitting the prunes on the top.

Bake for 30–35 minutes. Halfway through the cooking time, scatter the flaked almonds onto the tarts. When cooked, remove from the oven and allow to cool.

To serve, remove the tarts from their moulds and place on serving plates. Spoon the ice cream on the side.

Kentish pudding pie

I'm really passionate about desserts like Kentish pudding pie because they are some of the most threatened puddings in the UK – they should be on an endangered species list. Let's revive these traditional classics because, let's face it, we really love this type of pudding. Why do we go out to restaurants and enjoy the best of British for a starter and main course, then have to select a Continental-style dessert? Why can't we have a nice dollop of Kentish pudding pie and junket ice cream? (See page 73 for photograph.)

SERVES 6

500g sweet shortcrust pastry (see page 14)

2 eggs

75g caster sugar

150ml double cream

250ml milk

100g ground rice

pinch nutmeg

zest and juice of 1½ lemons

125g currants

icing sugar, to serve

TO SERVE:

junket ice cream (see page 182)

roasted crab apples (see page 72)

Make the pastry following the instructions on page 14.

Pre-heat the oven to 200°C/400°F/Gas mark 6. Line six 9cm tart tins with the pastry and blind-bake for 10–12 minutes. Remove from the oven and cool slightly.

Place the eggs and sugar into a bowl and whisk to combine.

Place the cream and milk into a saucepan and bring to a boil. Pour onto the eggs and sugar and whisk. Return to the saucepan and bring to a boil, stirring constantly. Cook until just thickened, then remove from the heat.

Whisk in the ground rice, nutmeg and lemon zest and juice. Pour into the tart cases. Sprinkle the currants over the custard.

Place the tarts onto a baking tray and bake for 10 minutes until just set and lightly golden. Serve with the roasted crab apples, junket ice cream and a dusting of icing sugar.

Spiced butternut squash tart

I love this recipe, and it's great served with the ginger and syrup ice cream on page 178. As with most tarts, don't overcook or the filling will split when cooling. You can also make this with pumpkin if you have trouble finding a squash.

SERVES 8

300g sweet shortcrust pastry (see page 14)

500g butternut squash, peeled and cut into large chunks

2 eggs

100g caster sugar

50g ground almonds

½ tsp ground cloves

½ tsp ground cinnamon

½ tsp ground ginger

½ tsp grated nutmeg

200ml single cream

icing sugar, for dusting

ginger and syrup ice cream (see page 178), for serving

Pre-heat the oven to190°C/375°F/Gas mark 5.

Roll out the pastry to a thickness of 5mm and line a 23cm loose-bottomed tart tin, then line with clingfilm or baking parchment and fill with baking beans or rice. Place on a baking tray and bake in the oven for 15 minutes.

Remove the clingfilm and baking beans and return to the oven for a further 10 minutes to crisp the base of the tart.

Meanwhile, place the butternut squash in a steamer over the top of a saucepan of boiling water and steam for 15–20 minutes until tender. Remove from the steamer and cool. Place the cooled squash into a food processor and blend to a purée.

Place the eggs and sugar in a large bowl and whisk to combine. Add the ground almonds, spices and single cream and whisk until smooth. Add the puréed squash and mix once more. Pour into the pastry tart and bake in the oven for 40–45 minutes until set. Remove from the oven and cool for at least 1 hour.

To make the cream, place the cream, syrup and ginger into a bowl and whisk until soft peaks are formed.

To serve, place a slice of tart on a plate with a spoonful of ginger and syrup ice cream and dust with icing sugar.

Pumpkin pie

Some people frown when they think of using veg in sweet dishes, but many vegetables work particularly well in desserts, such as butternut squash in ice cream, carrots in a carrot cake (see page 151), fennel with chocolate (see page 90), so why not pumpkin in a pie?

SERVES 8

FOR THE PASTRY:

175g plain flour, plus extra for rolling out

10g icing sugar

pinch of salt

75g butter, softened

40g pecans, roughly blitzed in a food processor

1 large egg yolk

1 egg white, lightly beaten

FOR THE FILLING:

450g (prepared weight) pumpkin flesh, cut into 2.5cm chunks

2 large eggs, plus 1 large yolk

1 tbsp molasses

75g soft dark brown sugar

1 tsp ground cinnamon

½ tsp freshly ground nutmeg

¼ tsp ground allspice

½ tsp ground cloves

½ tsp ground ginger

275ml double cream

For the pastry, sift the flour, icing sugar and salt into a large bowl. Add the butter and, using your fingertips, gently rub it into the flour. When the mixture is crumbly, add the chopped nuts, then sprinkle in 1–2 tbsp water and the egg yolk. Bring the pastry together (you may need to add more water) to make a smooth dough that will leave the bowl clean. Rest in the fridge for 30 minutes.

Cook the pumpkin in a steamer for 15–20 minutes, or until tender. Transfer to a blender and roughly purée.

Pre-heat the oven to 180°C/350°F/Gas mark 4. Lightly grease a 23cm, 4cm deep, loose-bottomed fluted tart tin.

Remove the pastry from the fridge and roll out on a floured surface. Transfer it, rolling it over the pin, to the tin. Press lightly all over the base and sides of the tin, easing any overlapping pastry back down the sides. Trim, leaving 5mm above the rim of the tin.

Prick the base all over with a fork and brush the pastry with the reserved egg white. Bake on a baking tray for 20–25 minutes until crisp and golden. (Check after 10 minutes – if the pastry has risen in the centre, prick it a few times and press it down again.)

For the filling, lightly whisk the eggs and extra yolk together in a large bowl. Place the molasses into a saucepan and heat gently. Add the sugar, spices and cream, then bring it up to simmering point, giving it a whisk to mix everything together. Pour it over the eggs and whisk again briefly. Add the pumpkin purée, still whisking to combine, then pour the filling into a jug.

When the pastry case is ready, remove it from the oven. Pour half the filling in, return the tart to the oven and, with the oven shelf half out, pour in the rest of the filling. Slide the shelf back in. Bake the pie for 35–40 minutes, or until puffed up round the edges but still slightly wobbly in the centre. Place the tin on a wire cooling rack. Serve chilled with crème fraîche.

Gooseberry crème fraîche tart

This just goes to prove that there is more to do with a gooseberry than a simple gooseberry fool. Not only is it a fantastic fruit for puddings, but it is particularly good for making into a chutney to serve with oily fish such as mackerel. Cooking with gooseberries brings back so many memories of my gran making gooseberry jam and chutney.

SERVES 6–8

butter, for greasing

200g sweet shortcrust pastry (see page 14)

flour, for rolling out

FOR THE FILLING:

200ml crème fraîche

4 large egg yolks

1 whole egg

100g caster sugar

450g gooseberries, topped and tailed

Pre-heat the oven to 190°C/375°F/Gas mark 5. Lightly grease a 23cm, 2.5cm deep, loose-bottomed tart tin.

Heat a baking tray in the oven while you roll out the pastry. Roll the pastry on a floured surface so that it is larger than the diameter of the tin. Line the tin with the pastry and prick the base all over with a fork. Brush the base and sides with some of the egg white leftover from the eggs for the filling. Place the pastry-lined tin on the hot baking tray (this will make the base cook).

Bake for 20 minutes until the pastry is just beginning to turn golden brown. Then remove it from the oven and reduce the heat to 180°C/350°F/Gas mark 4.

To make the filling, whisk the crème fraîche, yolks, whole egg and sugar together.

Carefully arrange the gooseberries in the pastry case, pour the crème fraîche mixture over the top and return the tart to the oven for 40–50 minutes or until it's a light golden brown. Allow to cool before serving.

Baked pear and honey tart

This tart is great served whole for a dinner party. The trick is not to put too much liquid in when cooking the pears as this will cause the tart to fall apart when portioned up. The cinnamon sauce on page 42 is fab with this.

SERVES 4–6

400g sweet shortcrust pastry (see page 14)

8 pears

caster sugar, to taste

20g unsalted butter, plus extra for greasing

4 medium egg yolks

1 medium whole egg

1 tbsp clear honey

600ml double cream

whipped cream, for serving

Pre-heat the oven to 180°C/350°F/Gas mark 4. Lightly grease a 24cm loose-bottomed tart tin.

Roll out the pastry into a circle 3mm thick and slightly wider than the tin. Line the tin, gently easing the pastry down into the corners. Leave 2.5cm pastry overhanging the edge. Chill for 10 minutes.

Line the pastry case with greaseproof paper and fill with dried beans, rice or flour. Put the tin onto a baking tray and bake for about 10 minutes. Remove the paper with the beans and bake the pastry case for a further 5 minutes, so that the pastry no longer looks glassy. Trim off the overhanging pastry edge level with the top of the tin.

Reduce the oven temperature to 170°C/325°F/Gas mark 3.

Peel, core and roughly slice six of the pears, Place in a pan with 1 tbsp water. Cook over a medium heat for 5–10 minutes, until soft. Sweeten with sugar to taste. Drain through a sieve to remove any excess liquid, then beat to a purée.

Peel and core the remaining two pears, and cut it into neat 6mm slices. Fry gently in the unsalted butter until softened and lightly coloured. Place the pear purée in the bottom of the pastry case and overlap the pear slices on top.

In a bowl, beat together the egg yolks, whole egg and honey, then whisk the double cream into the egg mix. Pour into the pastry case, over the pears, and bake for 30 minutes, until the mixture has set and is golden brown. Serve in slices with a dollop of cream.

Lemon meringue pie

This dessert is very popular in America and Australia, but in the UK it seems to carry the stigma of being a 1970s' restaurant dessert. However, when it's really well made, lemon meringue pie can hold its own against any other dessert served at the table.

SERVES 8

FOR THE PASTRY BASE:

110g cold unsalted butter, diced

225g plain white flour

a pinch of salt

2 tsp caster sugar

1 medium egg yolk

half an eggshell of cold water

FOR THE LEMON CURD:

zest and juice of 4 large lemons

5 tbsp cornflour

6 egg yolks

100g caster sugar

100g unsalted butter

FOR THE MERINGUE:

6 medium egg whites

300g caster sugar

Pre-heat the oven to 190°C/375°F/Gas mark 5. Grease a 23cm fluted loose-bottomed tin and place on a baking tray.

Make the pastry following the instructions for shortcrust pastry on page 14, then roll it out and line the tin.

Line the pastry case with greaseproof paper and fill with baking beans or flour. Blind-bake for 10 minutes. Remove from the oven and discard the greaseproof paper and flour or baking beans.

To make the lemon curd, bring 50ml water and the lemon juice to the boil in a saucepan. Dissolve the cornflour in a little water, then gradually pour the hot liquid onto the cornflour, whisking all the time until all incorporated and smooth. Return to the pan. Beat in the egg yolks, sugar and butter. Place back on the heat, add the zest and whisk for 30 seconds. Tip into the pastry case and leave to cool.

To make the meringue, follow the instructions for making hot meringue on page 34. Spoon the meringue into a piping bag with with a plain nozzle and pipe over the pastry case. Use a cook's blowtorch to colour the meringue, then serve.

Cakes and bakes

Madeira cake

Confusingly, Madeira cake does not come from the island of Madeira – it's an English cake, often called pound cake, dating back to the nineteenth century. It was always served with Madeira wine and now more often served with tea. Either way or on its own, it tastes great.

SERVES 10

175g butter, at room temperature

175g caster sugar

3 large eggs

250g self-raising flour

approximately 3 tbsp full-fat milk

finely grated zest of 1 lemon

icing sugar, for dusting

FOR THE CANDIED PEEL:

finely shredded peel of ½ lemon

50g sugar

Pre-heat the oven to 180°C/350°F/Gas mark 4. Grease an 18cm round cake tin, then line the base with greaseproof paper and grease the paper.

Cream the butter and sugar together in a bowl until pale and fluffy. Beat in the eggs, one at a time, beating the mixture well between each one and adding a tablespoon of the flour with the last egg to prevent the mixture from curdling.

Sift the flour and gently fold in with enough milk to give a mixture that falls reluctantly from the spoon. Fold in the lemon zest.

Spoon the mixture into the prepared tin and lightly level the top. Bake on the middle shelf of the oven for 45–50 minutes or until a warm skewer inserted into the centre comes out clean. Leave the cake to cool in the tin for 10 minutes, then turn it out onto a wire rack and leave to cool completely.

Meanwhile, make the candied peel. Dissolve the sugar in a saucepan with 50ml water, add the peel and simmer for 3–4 minutes. Remove from the heat and strain. Dust the cooled cake with icing sugar, then scatter the peel over the cake to decorate.

Butterfly cakes
I only ever see these cakes at village shows on the WI stands! If you're a complete beginner, this is where you want to start in this book as the recipe is so simple.

MAKES 12

175g unsalted butter, softened
175g caster sugar
few drops of vanilla extract
4 medium eggs
175g self-raising flour

FOR THE FILLING:

250ml double cream,
1 vanilla pod, split
icing sugar, for dusting

Pre-heat the oven to 180°C/350°F/Gas mark 4. Line a 12-hole cake tin with paper cases.

Cream the butter, sugar and vanilla essence together in a bowl until pale. Gradually add the eggs and beat to combine.

Sift the flour into the mixture and fold to combine. Spoon into the cases and bake in the pre-heated oven for 20–25 minutes, until golden brown and springy to the touch.

Remove from the oven and transfer to a wire rack to cool.

Meanwhile, whip the cream and vanilla seeds in a bowl to form soft peaks. Transfer to a piping bag fitted with a star nozzle.

Carefully slice off the domed tops of the fairy cakes. Cut the tops in half to form semi-circles and set aside. Pipe a little of the cream mixture onto the cut side of the cake. Press the two cake semi-circles into the cream, cut-side down, to create butterfly wings. Dust with icing sugar before serving.

Swiss roll

'Must try harder' were the words written in red ink over my old school cookery books, along with 'See me' and grades D- and F. Swiss roll was the second dish I learnt at school and I love making it even now. Oh, and to Mrs Baxter, my old school teacher, I'd like to say I did try harder.

SERVES 6–8

butter, for greasing

4 medium eggs

125g caster sugar, plus extra for dusting

few drops of vanilla extract

125g plain flour

FOR THE FILLING:

250ml double cream

½ vanilla pod, seeds only

150g strawberry or raspberry jam

Pre-heat the oven to 200°C/400°F/Gas mark 6. Grease a 2 x 22 x 32cm Swiss roll tin and line with greaseproof paper.

Place the eggs, half the sugar and vanilla essence into a bowl or food mixer and whisk until pale and thickened.

Place the remaining sugar on a baking tray and warm in the oven for a just few minutes. Once the egg and sugar mixture has thickened, add the warm sugar to the bowl and continue to whisk until combined.

Sift the flour into the bowl and fold together. Pour the sponge mixture into the prepared tin and bake for 10–12 minutes, until golden and springy to the touch.

Place a sheet of greaseproof paper on a damp tea towel and dust generously with caster sugar. Turn the sponge out onto the paper and remove the base lining. Leave to cool.

For the filling, whip the cream with the seeds from the vanilla pod. Spread the jam over the cake, then spread a layer of cream on top. Carefully roll up with the aid of the paper. Make sure the first turn is tight so the cake will roll evenly.

Transfer the Swiss roll to a serving plate and dust with caster sugar before serving.

Chocolate fudge cake

Chocolate fudge cake is the recipe for the chocoholic in everyone. It's rich, dark and, sadly, one of those cakes where after eating one slice, you just want another – a bit like a packet of chocolate digestives, or is that just me?

SERVES 6–8

FOR THE CAKE:

175g very soft butter, plus extra for greasing

175g self-raising wholemeal flour

1 rounded tbsp cocoa powder

1 rounded tsp baking powder

175g light soft brown sugar

3 large eggs, at room temperature

FOR THE FILLING AND TOPPING:

125g light soft brown sugar

170g tin of evaporated milk

125g dark chocolate (50–55% cocoa solids), broken into small pieces

50g butter, softened

2 drops vanilla extract

TO DECORATE:

flaked almonds

cocoa powder or icing sugar, for dusting

Pre-heat the oven to 170°C/325°F/Gas mark 3. Lightly grease a 20cm springform cake tin and line the base with baking parchment.

Weigh the flour, then take out 1 rounded tbsp and replace it with the rounded tbsp of cocoa. (The tablespoon of flour you remove won't be needed.)

Add the baking powder to the flour and cocoa, tip into a bowl, add the remaining cake ingredients and beat them together. You will end up with a mixture that drops off a spoon when you give it a whack on the side of the bowl. If the mixture seems a little too stiff, add a little water and mix again.

Spread the mixture evenly in the prepared tin and bake on the centre shelf of the oven for about 40–45 minutes or until springy in the centre. Remove from the oven and, after about 30 seconds, turn the cake out onto a wire cooling rack and strip off the base papers. Once cool, carefully cut the cake in half horizontally and set aside.

For the filling, combine the sugar and evaporated milk in a heavy saucepan. Heat gently to dissolve the sugar, stirring frequently. When the sugar has dissolved and the mixture comes to the boil, keep the heat very low and simmer for 6 minutes without stirring. Remove the pan from the heat and, using a small balloon whisk, whisk in the chocolate, followed by the butter and vanilla essence.

Transfer the mixture to a bowl and, when it is cool, cover it with clingfilm and chill for about 1 hour to allow the mixture to thicken. Then beat again and spread half on one sponge, placing the other sponge on top. Spread the remainder over the top and sides. Decorate the top with the almonds and dust with cocoa powder or icing sugar to serve.

Sachertorte

This is a rich, Austrian chocolate cake invented in 1832 by Franz Sacher in a hotel in Vienna. It is probably one of the most famous Viennese specialities. Traditionally, it would be eaten with whipped cream, but for me, pouring cream is delicious as well.

SERVES 8

FOR THE CAKE:

110g soft butter, plus extra for greasing

175g dark chocolate

110g caster sugar

4 large egg yolks, lightly beaten

a dash of vanilla extract

125g plain flour

½ tsp baking powder

5 large egg whites

FOR THE ICING:

4 tsp smooth apricot jam

175g dark chocolate

150ml double cream

2 tsp glucose

Pre-heat the oven to 150°C/300°F/Gas mark 2. Lightly grease a 20cm springform cake tin and line the base with baking parchment.

Melt the chocolate slowly in a heatproof bowl set over a saucepan of barely simmering water (make sure the base of the bowl doesn't touch the water).

Using an electric hand whisk, cream the butter and sugar until very pale and fluffy. Beat in the egg yolks a little at a time, whisking well after each addition.

When the chocolate has cooled slightly, fold it gradually into the creamed butter mixture and then add the vanilla. Add the flour and baking powder and carefully fold it in with a large metal spoon.

Whisk the egg whites in a large, clean bowl to the stiff-peak stage which will take a few minutes, then carefully fold them into the mixture, little by little, using a metal spoon.

Pour the mixture into the prepared cake tin, level the top and bake on the middle shelf of the oven for about 1 hour, or until firm and well risen. When cooked, allow the cake to cool in the tin for 10 minutes before turning it out onto a cooling rack, then leave it to get quite cold.

Warm the apricot jam and brush the cake all over with it.

To make the icing, melt the chocolate with cream, also in a bowl over simmering water. Then remove the bowl from the heat and stir in the glucose to give a coating consistency. Pour the icing over the whole cake, making sure it covers the top and sides completely. Leave to set for a few hours before serving.

Wedding cake

You will never make enough chocolate curls to decorate this cake so order them from a chocolate supplier (see mail-order addresses on page 188). You may also wish to order a small bouquet of flowers from a florist, to place on top of the cake.

SERVES 25–30

FOR THE LARGE SPONGE:
700g butter, plus extra for greasing
700g caster sugar
12 medium eggs
650g self-raising flour

FOR THE SMALL SPONGE:
275g butter
275g caster sugar
6 medium eggs
275g self-raising flour

FOR THE BUTTERCREAM:
500g unsalted butter, softened
500g icing sugar

FOR THE DECORATION:
2 boxes of chocolate curls
small roses in a variety of colours
ivy leaves
5cm block of florists' oasis, covered
   in foil

Pre-heat the oven to 180°C/350°F/Gas mark 4.

For the large sponge, lightly butter a 30cm cake tin and line the base with greaseproof paper. Cream the butter and sugar until smooth and pale in colour and then gradually beat in the eggs. Sift the flour and fold into the mixture, a little at a time. Pour into the cake tin, level off the mixture with a palette knife and bake for about 1½ hours or until a skewer inserted into the cake comes out clean. Cool on a wire rack.

For the small sponge, lightly butter a 24cm cake tin and line the base with greaseproof paper. Mix the sponge in the same way but only bake for about 45 minutes.

To assemble the cake, place the large sponge cake onto a cake board, serving plate or cake stand, then position the smaller sponge cake centrally on top.

To make the buttercream, beat the butter and icing sugar together in a large bowl until almost a white. Spread the buttercream generously over both cakes. Stick the chocolate curls upright around the edge of each cake.

Push the stems of the roses and ivy into the foil-covered oasis to make a pretty arrangement. Carefully place the flower arrangement on top of the cake, securing it with cocktail sticks if necessary.

Carrot cake

The idea of decorating the cake in this way comes from a French method of cooking carrots. Boil them quickly so they cook in the evaporating water, leaving a buttery, sugary glaze in the pan to swirl the cooked carrots in.

SERVES 8

FOR THE CAKE:

200g carrots, peeled and coarsely grated

175g dark soft brown sugar

2 large eggs

150ml olive oil (not virgin olive oil)

200g wholemeal self-raising flour

1 tbsp ground mixed spice

1 tsp bicarbonate of soda

80g pecans, roughly chopped

grated zest of 1 lemon

110g sultanas

25g raisins

50g desiccated coconut

FOR THE ICING:

250g mascarpone

250ml double cream

2 tbsp icing sugar

FOR THE CARROT DECORATION:

300g baby carrots (washed)

1 tsp salt

70g sugar

50g butter

FOR THE BANANA TUILES:

1 ripe banana, peeled and roughly chopped

1 medium egg white

TO DECORATE:

pulled sugar (see pages 32–33)

Pre-heat the oven to 190°C/375°F/Gas mark 5. Lightly grease a 25cm, 6cm deep cake tin and line the base with baking parchment.

To make the cake, whisk the sugar, eggs and oil together in a bowl with an electric hand whisk for 3–4 minutes until smooth. Now sift the flour, mixed spice and bicarbonate of soda into the bowl, tipping in any bits left in the sieve. Stir together gently, then add the remaining cake ingredients.

Pour the cake mixture evenly into the tin and bake on the centre shelf of the oven for 35–40 minutes. It should be nicely risen and feel firm and springy to the touch when lightly pressed in the centre. If not, give it another few minutes and test again. Remove the cake from the tin and cool on a wire rack.

Make the icing by mixing all the ingredients together in a bowl until light and fluffy. Cover with clingfilm and leave in the fridge until you are ready to ice the cake.

To make the glazed carrots, trim the green carrot stalks to 2.5cm in length. Place the carrots in a saucepan and just cover with cold water. Add the salt, sugar and butter, bring to the boil and boil quickly for 5–6 minutes. The carrots will cook as the water evaporates, and a glaze is formed in the bottom of the pan. Coat in the glaze, remove from the pan and leave to cool.

To make the banana tuiles, purée the banana in a mini blender, add the egg white and whiz together. Spread the batter onto silicone paper on a baking tray in a very thin layer in the desired shapes (see page 22 for template instructions). Bake in the oven at 180°C/350°F/Gas mark 4 for 20–30 minutes until brown. Remove the tuiles from the tray while still hot and leave to cool.

To decorate, spread the icing roughly over the top of the cake. Garnish the top with the banana tuiles, sugared carrots and lengths of pulled sugar.

Fire-and-ice cake

The reason I call this fire-and-ice cake is because the tuile biscuits resemble flickering flames, while the buttercream looks like ice. You can use different flowers for the top of the cake, but do make sure they have dramatic shapes and colours.

SERVES 15–20

3 quantities of Victoria sponge mixture (see page 19)

1 quantity of tuile biscuit mixture (see page 22)

1kg unsalted butter, softened

350g icing sugar

jar of apricot purée

TO DECORATE:

heliconia stricta flower

bird of paradise flower

calla lilies

hazel twigs

strawberries, hulled and cut in half

1 fig, cut into quarters

kumquats, cut in half

small block of florists' oasis, covered in foil

Grease and flour three round cake tins (you will need one 18cm, one 20cm and one 25cm tin). Make up the sponge mixture following the recipe on page 19 and divide it between the three tins. Bake as instructed, but bear in mind the small cake will need slightly less time in the oven and the large cake slightly more.

Pre-heat the oven to 200°C/400°F/Gas mark 6. Cut three templates from margarine tub lids in the shape of a flame – small, medium and large. Following the tuile recipe on page 22, use a palette knife to spread the mixture very thinly over the template onto a baking tray lined with non-stick baking parchment, then lift the template off. Bake in the oven for 3–4 minutes, until lightly golden.

Remove from the oven. To create the curved flame shape, you will need to place the warm tuiles over two cylindrical objects of slightly different diameters (a rolling pin and the cardboard tube from a roll of kitchen paper work well). Place the wider end of the tuile over the larger object, and the pointed end over the smaller one. As the tuiles cool, they will take on the curved shape. Continue this process until you have approximately 15–20 tuiles in each size.

To make the buttercream, beat the icing sugar and butter to an almost white batter. Slice each sponge in half horizontally and spread with a little of the buttercream and apricot purée. Sandwich the sponges together again.

Place the large sponge on a cake board with the medium one on top and the small one on the top of that.

Spread the remaining buttercream evenly over the sponges and position the tuile biscuits around the edges of each cake (the buttercream will hold them in place).

Place the flowers, twigs and leaves into some foil-covered oasis and place on the top of the cake. Secure with cocktail sticks if necessary. Scatter the strawberries, figs and kumquats around the top of the cake to finish.

Gâteau Saint-Honoré

For me, you can't really have a dessert book without featuring this cake. The name comes from Honorius, the patron saint of bakers and confectioners who lived in France in the seventh century. This classic dessert is seen in French pâtisseries. It's a choux pastry base with choux pastry profiteroles arranged around the edge. The last time I had it, it was filled with a mixture of crème pâtissière and double cream. I make mine with custard and double cream, but you still get the same flavour and effect.

SERVES 8–10

1 quantity of choux pastry (see pages 16–17)

300ml double cream

200ml fresh custard

1 vanilla pod, seeds only

100g caster sugar

50ml orange liqueur

TO GARNISH:

10–12 small white and pink roses

small twisted twigs

Pre-heat the oven to 180°C/350°F/Gas mark 4. Line two baking trays with parchment. Place a 23cm metal ring on one of the lined trays.

Make the choux pastry recipe as on pages 16–17. Transfer the pastry to a piping bag, and use half to pipe into 12 small buns on one of the baking trays. Pipe the remaining half into the metal ring on the other baking tray. Transfer the baking trays to the oven and cook for 10–15 minutes, until risen and golden. Set aside to cool.

Next, whip up the double cream until firm, split the vanilla pod and add the seeds only to the cream. Fold the custard into the cream together with 2 tbsp of the sugar and a dash of orange liqueur.

Heat the remaining sugar in a non-stick pan over a medium heat and cook to a caramel. If the mixture begins to set, warm up gently.

Once the sugar has been caramelized, carefully dip each choux bun into the sugar and then place on a greased baking tray to cool.

Remove the ring from the pastry base and drizzle the remaining liqueur over the middle. Using an ice cream scoop or a tablespoon warmed in hot water, place half the custard and cream mixture into the centre of the base.

Use the remaining cream mixture to fill the choux buns and arrange the buns around the edge of the flan. Garnish one side with the roses and twigs and serve.

Grandma's caramel shortbread

It's not just my gran who should be thanked for this recipe – it's a chap called Gale Borden who invented condensed milk. While sailing to the UK from the US in the 1850s, the cows in the ship's hold became too sick to be milked so the supply of fresh milk dried up. Several sailors subsequently died from drinking milk that had been stored onboard for too long and this led to Borden developing condensed milk as we know it.

MAKES ABOUT 6

1 x 397g tin of condensed milk

250g unsalted butter, at room temperature

150g caster sugar

150g cornflour

300g flour

First, make the caramel. Place the tin of condensed milk in a deep saucepan and cover it with water. Bring to the boil, then reduce the heat and cover with a lid. Leave to simmer rapidly for 2 hours (keep an eye on the water level). Allow it to cool completely before you open the tin where you'll find a golden sticky caramel. (Once cooked, a tin of caramelized condensed milk will keep in the fridge for 2 weeks.)

Pre-heat the oven to 170°C/340°F/Gas mark 3½. Line a 20 x 30cm baking tin with baking parchment.

Cream the butter with the sugar until light and fluffy. Sift together the flours, then mix with the cream and sugar. Gently knead the dough until it comes together in a firm ball.

Roll out two-thirds of the dough to fit the tin and lay it inside, pressing it neatly into the edges. Spread three-quarters of the condensed milk caramel evenly over the base. Crumble the remaining dough over the top of the caramel.

Bake for 20 minutes. The caramel should bubble up a little between the dough and the top of the shortbread should be golden. Leave to cool in the tin for 5 minutes, then cut into squares. Finish cooling in the tin.

To serve, re-heat the squares for 5 minutes at 160°C/325°F/Gas mark 3. Finish with a sprig of fresh mint, a dollop of vanilla ice cream and a drizzle of the remaining caramel sauce.

Lardy cake

I live in Hampshire and the next county to me is Wiltshire, home of the lardy cake. For me, this is where the best lardy cake are to be found – most bakers sell it crammed with as much fruit, sugar and lard as they can. Forget the diet and just dive in.

SERVES 6

15g fresh yeast

275ml warm water

450g strong white flour

2 pinches of salt

75g lard, diced

75g butter, diced

100g sultanas

75g currants

50g chopped mixed peel

50g caster sugar

Blend the fresh yeast with the warm water (don't use hot water as this would kill the yeast; cold water can be used but the dough would take longer to prove).

Put the flour and salt in a bowl and rub in one-third of the lard. Make a well in the centre and pour in the yeast liquid. Mix together to make a dough that leaves the sides of the bowl clean (add a bit more water if necessary).

Turn onto a lightly floured surface and knead well for about 5 minutes, until smooth and elastic. Place in a clean bowl. Cover with a clean tea towel and leave in a warm place for about 1 hour, until doubled in size.

Turn the dough onto a floured surface and roll out to a rectangle about 5mm thick. Dot one-third of the remaining lard and one-third of the butter over the surface of the dough. Sprinkle over one-third of the fruit, peel and sugar. Fold the dough in three, folding the bottom third up and the top third down. Give a quarter turn, then repeat the process twice more, using up the remaining ingredients.

Grease a 20 x 25cm baking tin. Roll the dough out to fit the prepared tin. Place into the tin, cover and leave in a warm place for 30 minutes until it rises.

Pre-heat the oven to 220°C/425°F/Gas mark 7. Score the top of the dough in a criss-cross pattern using a very sharp knife, then bake in the oven for about 30 minutes until golden brown. Turn out and serve warm.

Chocolate cola cake

Everyone who knows me knows I am sucker for drinking diet cola and snacking on chocolate bars. This recipe sounds odd but it tastes great and is so moist when cooked – I love it. If you prefer a thicker frosting, double the quantities for the topping.

SERVES 8

250g butter, plus extra for greasing

250g self-raising flour

300g golden caster sugar

3 heaped tbsp cocoa

generous pinch of bicarbonate of soda

200ml cola drink

75ml milk

2 eggs, beaten

1 tsp vanilla extract

FOR THE TOPPING:

60g butter, softened

200g icing sugar, sifted

2–3 tbsp cocoa

2 tbsp cola drink

FOR THE SAUCE:

king-sized caramel chocolate bar

splash of double cream

2 tbsp mini marshmallows (optional)

Pre-heat the oven to 180°C/350°F/Gas mark 4. Grease a 24cm loose-bottomed cake tin.

Sift the flour, sugar, cocoa and bicarbonate of soda into a bowl. Gently melt the butter and cola drink together in a pan, then add to the dry ingredients, together with the milk, eggs and vanilla extract. Mix gently but thoroughly, then tip into the cake tin.

Bake for about 40 minutes or until a skewer inserted into the centre of the cake comes out clean. Remove from the oven and leave to cool on a wire rack for about 15 minutes while you make the topping.

To make the topping, beat the butter, icing sugar and cocoa together in a bowl until blended. Beat in the cola to combine. Spread over the cake and allow the topping to set.

To make the sauce, melt the chocolate bar gently in a pan with a splash of cream (you may want to add a little warm water to achieve a pouring consistency), then stir in the marshmallows if using. The sauce is rich and sweet, as is the topping, so you may want to serve with one or the other rather than both.

Macadamia nut chocolate cake

I don't know why macadamia nuts aren't as popular as they should be – most people seem to opt for a combination of chocolate and hazelnut. These individual cakes must be served warm as they become more like a muffin when eaten cold. If necessary, give them a quick blast in the microwave for 10 seconds to bring them back to full glory.

SERVES 6

75g toasted macadamia nuts
190g unsalted butter
200g sugar
4 eggs
45g unsweetened cocoa, sifted
70g plain flour
¼ tsp baking powder

FOR THE CHOCOLATE SAUCE:
25g bittersweet chocolate, chopped
1 tbsp unsalted butter
4 tbsp double cream
15g sugar

TO SERVE:
coconut ice cream (see page 179)

Pre-heat the oven to 180°C/350°F/Gas mark 4. Butter 6 ring moulds 5cm wide by 2.5cm deep. Place on a parchment-lined baking tray.

Finely grind half the macadamia nuts and coarsely chop the remaining half.

Cream the butter and sugar together and add the eggs one at a time, mixing well after each addition. Add the cocoa, flour and baking powder and stir until fully incorporated. Gently fold the ground nuts into the batter.

Fill the moulds two-thirds full with the batter and sprinkle with the chopped macadamia nuts.

Bake for 15–20 minutes or until a skewer inserted into the centre comes out clean.

To make the sauce, gently heat the chocolate and butter in a saucepan until melted, stir in the cream and sugar and continue to heat gently, stirring, until combined.

To serve, pour a pool of chocolate sauce onto each plate. Place a cake in the centre of each plate on top of the sauce. Spoon the ice cream to the side.

Chocolate chip cookies

I call this 'pastry chef's chewing gum' as I used to eat masses of this raw dough while working – strange, I know! I used to mould the soft mixture into balls and place them on a baking tray to firm up in the fridge, then once cold pile into a container and store in the fridge for up to a week. Whenever you want fresh cookies, take a ball, place onto the tray and bake.

MAKES 30

110g butter, softened
110g light muscovado sugar
1 vanilla pod, seeds only
1 medium egg, lightly beaten
75g plain wholemeal flour
110g dark chocolate chips
50g toasted hazelnuts, chopped

Pre-heat the oven to 180°C/350°F/Gas mark 4. Line two 28 x 35cm baking trays with baking parchment.

Place the butter and sugar in a mixing bowl and beat together with an electric hand whisk until light and fluffy.

Split the vanilla pod lengthways. Using the end of a teaspoon or a small sharp knife, scoop out the seeds. Beat the egg and the vanilla seeds into the mixture, then add the remaining ingredients and stir until thoroughly mixed.

Take spoonfuls of the dough (about the size of a walnut) and arrange them on the baking trays, spaced well apart.

Bake them on the shelf just above the centre of the oven for 10 minutes or until the cookies have turned a golden colour and feel firm in the centre when lightly pressed.

As soon as the cookies are baked, remove then from the baking sheets using a palette knife. Cool them on a wire rack and, when cold, store in an airtight container.

Dark chocolate brownies

There are stacks of brownie recipes around. This one originally came from an old American pastry chef I once knew. If you have any broken brownies leftover, mix them into some vanilla ice cream or sprinkle them over the top when serving.

MAKES 10–12

250g unsalted butter, plus extra for greasing

100g plain flour, sieved, plus extra for flouring tin

350g dark chocolate

3 medium eggs

250g dark muscovado sugar

1 tsp baking powder

pinch of salt

Pre-heat the oven to 170°C/325°F/Gas mark 3. Grease and flour a 23cm square cake tin. Line the base with greaseproof paper.

Melt the butter and chocolate together in a heatproof bowl set over a pan of simmering water.

Whisk the eggs together and slowly add the sugar. Beat in the chocolate mixture and gently fold in the flour, baking powder and pinch of salt.

Pour the mixture into the tin. Bake in the oven for 40–45 minutes until the surface is set. It is cooked when a skewer placed in the middle comes out with a little of the mixture sticking to it.

Remove from the oven and cool in the tin slightly, then place on a wire rack and leave to cool.

Cut the cake into squares and keep in a tin or in the fridge.

Buttermilk scones

I first came across buttermilk about five years ago, and my chefs from India use it a lot in desserts and breads. It's the liquid leftover from the churning process of making butter using full-fat milk and has a slightly sour taste. Buttermilk can be used as an alternative to milk when making cakes and in baking in general. Make these scones by hand, rather than using a food processor as this would produce a tougher dough.

MAKES ABOUT 10

75g butter, at room temperature, plus extra for greasing

225g self-raising flour, plus a little extra for rolling out and dusting

pinch of salt

40g caster sugar

1 large egg, beaten

2 tbsp buttermilk, plus a little extra for brushing

clotted cream and jam, for serving

Pre-heat the oven to 220°C/425°F/Gas mark 7. Lightly grease a baking tray.

Sift the flour and salt into a bowl, rub the butter lightly into the mixture until it looks like breadcrumbs, then add the sugar. Beat the egg and 2 tbsp of the buttermilk together in another bowl, then start to add this to the flour mixture, mixing the dough with a palette knife. When it begins to come together, finish off with your hands – it should be soft but not sticky

When you have formed the dough into a ball, tip it on to a lightly floured surface and roll it into a circle at least 2.5cm thick – be very careful not to roll it any thinner as the secret of well-risen scones is to start off with a thickness of no less than 2.5cm.

Cut out the scones by placing a 5cm plain edge cutter on the dough and giving it a sharp tap – don't twist it, just lift it up and push the dough out. Carry on until you are left with the trimmings, then bring these back together to roll out again so you can cut out one last scone.

Turn the scones over and place on the baking tray, brush them lightly with buttermilk and dust with a little flour. Bake on the top shelf of the oven for 10–12 minutes or until they are well risen and golden brown, then remove them to a wire rack to cool.

Serve with clotted cream and any jam or jelly that takes your fancy.

Jam shortbreads

This shortbread is very wet and is almost like a bun mixture before baking, but this will make the biscuits very light in texture, and they just dissolve in the mouth. They're very moreish, too.

MAKES 20–24

90g icing sugar
185g plain flour
60g cornflour
30g ground almonds
250g butter, cut into cubes
½ tsp almond essence
caster sugar, for dusting
raspberry or strawberry jam

Pre-heat the oven to 180°C/350°F/Gas mark 4.

Sift the icing sugar, flour and cornflour together into a bowl. Add the ground almonds and butter. Using your fingers, a mixer or food processor, rub or mix the butter in until there are no visible lumps of butter.

Add the almond essence. Turn the mixture out onto a lightly floured surface and knead a few times, just to form a smooth dough.

Cover a baking tray with a non-stick baking mat and place a 6cm metal ring on top. Roll the dough into 20–24 small balls and place one inside the metal ring, push it down and flatten the top slightly with your fingers. Repeat with the remaining dough.

Bake the shortbreads for 8–12 minutes until they are a light golden colour. Remove them from the oven and using a round kitchen tool, such as the end of a wooden spoon handle, make a small indentation in the top of each biscuit.

Let the shortbreads cool for a few minutes, then neaten the edges of the biscuits by re-cutting with the metal ring. Be gentle, as they are fragile while they are still warm. Transfer to a wire rack to cool.

When cooled, dust the tops with some icing sugar in a shaker or sieve. Using a teaspoon, fill the indentation with a little jam or your chosen filling.

Apple and toffee muffins

Don't put too much toffee in each of the muffins or it will boil over during baking. For a different flavour, try using nutmeg instead of cinnamon. These muffins also make a great pudding when served with vanilla ice cream.

MAKES 12

2 eggs, beaten

80g castor sugar

240ml milk

100g butter, melted

300g plain flour

2 tsp baking powder

½ tsp salt

good pinch of cinnamon

2 eating apples, such as Cox's or Granny Smiths, peeled, cored and finely chopped

50g toffee, broken into small pieces

Pre-heat the oven to 190°C/375°F/Gas mark 5. Line a 12-hole bun or muffin tin with paper cases.

Mix the eggs, sugar, milk and melted butter in a large bowl. Sift in the flour, baking powder, salt and cinnamon. Add the chopped apple and mix roughly.

Spoon the mixture into the muffin cases, filling them a quarter full, then top with a few pieces of toffee, and cover with the rest of the muffin mixture until the paper cases are half full.

Bake in the oven for 30–35 minutes until well risen and golden. Cool on a wire rack.

Ice creams and sorbets

Chocolate sorbet

The most important advice I can give you when buying chocolate for cooking is to buy the best you can afford, but don't go for sweet chocolate bars.

SERVES 4

200ml milk
100g caster sugar
50g liquid glucose
20g cocoa powder
160g dark chocolate, chopped

Place the milk, sugar, glucose and cocoa in a saucepan with 200ml water.

Heat gently, whisking all the time, until the mixture boils, then add the chopped chocolate.

Allow the chocolate to melt, then pass the mixture through a sieve and allow to cool.

When cool, churn in an ice-cream machine until set.

Once frozen, transfer the sorbet from the machine into a freezerproof container with a lid and store in the freezer. The sorbet will keep for a few months.

Brown bread ice cream
Who would have thought that brown bread in desserts would add so much flavour, yet it's the bread that makes this ice cream taste so good.

SERVES 4–6

175g brown wholemeal
  breadcrumbs
300ml double cream
300ml single cream
125g icing sugar
2 egg yolks
1 tbsp rum (optional)
2 egg whites

Pre-heat the oven to 200°C/400°F/Gas mark 6.

Spread the breadcrumbs out on a baking tray and toast in the oven for a couple of minutes until crisp and slightly browned.

Meanwhile, beat the two creams with the sugar. Mix together the yolks and rum, if using, and add to the cream mixture, beating it in well.

When the breadcrumbs are cool, fold them gently into the cream mixture, making sure they are evenly distributed.

Lastly, whip the whites of the eggs until stiff and fold into the mixture. Transfer to a sealable container, place in the freezer and store until needed. (There is no need to stir this ice cream while it freezes.)

Vanilla ice cream

This standard recipe for ice cream can be adapted to make different flavours simply by removing the vanilla pod and replacing with zest and juice, or a juicy fruit such as passion fruit. However, if you are making a honey- or alcohol-flavoured ice cream, remove 50g of sugar from this recipe as too much sugar or alcohol will act as a defrosting agent.

SERVES 6–8

1 vanilla pod
500ml milk
200g caster sugar
500ml double cream
8 egg yolks

Using a sharp knife, cut the vanilla pod in half lengthways and remove the seeds. Place the milk, vanilla seeds and pod, half the caster sugar and the cream in a pan and bring to the boil.

Whisk the egg yolks in a bowl and add the remaining sugar. When the cream mixture has boiled, pour it slowly on to the eggs, whisking all the time. Return the mixture to the pan over a high heat and mix quickly until the mixture has thickened.

Pass through a sieve into a bowl, then place the mixture into an ice-cream machine. Churn until the ice cream has set.

Once set, transfer the ice cream into a sealable container, place in the freezer and store until needed.

To make the almond ice cream featured on page 75, reduce the quantity of caster sugar to 150g and add 75–100ml amaretto and 50g toasted flaked almonds.

White chocolate ice cream

This has to be one of my favourite ice creams. It's smooth and tastes so good either on its own, with fruit or served simply with chocolate sauce. Make sure you use good-quality white chocolate and not standard sweet bars of white chocolate as these are full of other ingredients which will cause the mixture to go grainy in texture when churned.

SERVES 6–8

12 egg yolks
200g caster sugar
600ml milk
250g white chocolate, chopped
600ml double cream

Whisk the egg yolks and caster sugar together in a bowl until pale and fluffy.

Bring the milk up to the boil in a pan.

Place the chocolate into a large bowl and leave to one side.

Pour the hot milk onto the egg yolks and whisk together. Return to the pan and heat, stirring all the time until the mixture thickens.

Pass the hot mixture through a sieve onto the chocolate and allow to cool.

Mix in the cream and place in an ice-cream machine and churn until set. Transfer to a sealable container, place in the freezer and store until needed.

Ginger and syrup ice cream

Don't be fooled by the lack of ingredients here – it's the addition of the syrup that will stop the ice cream setting like rock. The first time I made this was in the kitchens of Castle Howard when I was aged about 12. It was great then and is fab now. It's so simple to make and you don't even need an ice-cream machine. Also, it's thought that this is how ice cream was first invented by the Chinese some 2,000 years ago. At that time, ice cream was just a mixture of snow and honey.

SERVES 4

200ml double cream

3 tbsp stem ginger syrup

25g stem ginger, finely chopped

Simply place the double cream, syrup and chopped ginger in a bowl and whisk until soft peaks are formed.

Pour the mixture into a sealable container, place in the freezer and freeze until required.

Coconut ice cream

All the ice creams and sorbets in this chapter are made slightly differently for a reason. In this coconut recipe I have used a method which produces a beautifully creamy texture.

SERVES 6–8

400ml double cream

300ml coconut cream

300ml milk

6 egg yolks

225g caster sugar

60g desiccated coconut

50ml white rum or coconut liqueur, such as Malibu

Place the double cream, coconut cream and milk into a saucepan and bring to the boil.

Place the egg yolks and sugar into a bowl and whisk until light and thickened.

Pour the hot milk mixture onto the eggs, whisking continuously until the mixture is smooth. Pour it back into saucepan and bring to nearly simmering point, stirring constantly, until thickened (but don't boil).

Pour the custard into a bowl and stir in the desiccated coconut and white rum or coconut liqueur.

Leave to cool, then churn in an ice-cream machine until frozen. Transfer into a sealable container and place in the freezer until ready to serve.

Fresh mango sorbet

This recipe will also work well with strawberries and many other fruits that can be made into a purée. Whichever fruit you choose, do use the lemon juice as it adds to the taste. In total, you will need about 900ml of liquid purée for this quantity of sugar. If you want a softer style of sorbet, add a whipped egg white to the mix when the churning stage is nearly complete.

SERVES 6–8

3 fresh mangoes

200g icing sugar, sifted

juice of 2 lemons

Peel and stone the mangoes. Dice the flesh into pieces and place in a blender or food processor. Add the icing sugar and lemon juice and blend to a purée.

Place into an ice cream machine and churn to freeze.

Once frozen, transfer from the machine into a sealable container and store in the freezer until required. The sorbet will keep for a few months.

Junket ice cream

Junket is such an old-fashioned dish. Roughly speaking, it is made from warmed milk with rennet added and allowed to set, sometimes flavoured with rum or vanilla. Here I've taken the flavours and milk and made it into ice cream. Served with other old classic puds like spotted dick (see page 56) and Kentish pudding pie (see page 128), it tastes great.

SERVES 10

8 eggs
180g caster sugar
250ml double cream
750ml milk
1 vanilla pod
6 tbsp rum

Place the eggs and sugar into a bowl and whisk to combine.

Place the cream, milk and split vanilla pod into a saucepan and bring to a boil. Pour onto the eggs and sugar and whisk.

Return to the saucepan and bring to a boil, stirring constantly. Cook for about 1 minute, until just thickened, then remove from the heat. Pass the mixture through a sieve into a bowl and add the rum.

Pour into an ice-cream machine and churn until frozen.

Transfer the mixture to a sealable container, place in the freezer and freeze until required.

Lemon granita

Granita is related to sorbet as it's a semi-frozen dessert made from water, sugar and flavourings. It originates from Italy and that's where I've eaten some of the best granitas, probably due to the quality of the lemons. The texture of granitas varies so much – if churned in a machine it will become smoother, but if forked through it will have a chunkier texture.

SERVES 6

250g caster sugar
zest of 2 lemons
juice of 4 lemons

Put the caster sugar into a saucepan with 500ml water and bring to the boil. Simmer for 5 minutes, then leave to cool.

Add the lemon zest and juice to the sugar syrup.

Pour into a freezerproof container and freeze for 3 hours, stirring every 15 minutes to prevent the mixture freezing into a solid block.

20-second strawberry ice cream

If there is such a thing as no-fat ice cream, this has to be it. An extra bonus is that it's so quick to make. The only down side is that it doesn't refreeze once made. Freeze the whole strawberries on a baking tray so that you have separate frozen fruits, rather than a solid block of them.

SERVES 6–8

400g whole strawberries, with the green removed and frozen (see recipe introduction above)

dash of vanilla extract

30g caster sugar

150ml buttermilk

200g mixed berries, to serve (optional)

Tip the frozen strawberry pieces into a food processor. Add the vanilla extract, sugar and half the buttermilk.

Turn on the processor and let it run for a few moments. Then, while it is still running, pour in the remaining buttermilk in a thin, steady stream. Let the machine run until the mixture is beautifully smooth and creamy. Don't overmix as this will cause the ice cream to defrost.

Serve straight away with mixed fresh berries.

Apple sorbet

Compared to the other recipes in this chapter, this is a very different way of making a sorbet, but this method produces a very fresh flavour.

SERVES 6

4 large Granny Smith apples

juice of 1 large lemon

200g caster sugar

4 tbsp liquid glucose

Quarter and core the apples, but do not peel. Toss them in a bowl with the lemon juice. Place in a single layer in a shallow plastic container and freeze for at least 1 hour.

Dissolve the sugar in 400ml water in a heavy-based saucepan over a low heat. Bring to the boil and cook over a medium heat for 5 minutes. Cool, then mix in the glucose.

Whiz the ice-cold apples in a food processor, gradually adding about a third of the syrup to make a fine purée. Scrape down the sides of the bowl once or twice as you do this. Mix in the rest of the syrup.

Transfer the mixture to an ice-cream machine. Churn until almost solid, then transfer to a rigid plastic container, seal and freeze until required. Serve in scoops.

Useful addresses

Index

SPECIALIST KITCHEN EQUIPMENT

Nisbets
Fourth Way
Avonmouth
Bristol BS11 8TB
0845 140 5555
www.nisbets.co.uk

Pages Catering
121 Shaftesbury Avenue
London WC2H 8AD
0845 373 4017
www.pagescatering.co.uk

Hansens Kitchen Equipment
306 Fulham Road
London SW10 9ER
020 7351 6933
www.shoppingathansens.co.uk

Leon Jaeggi
77 Shaftesbury Avenue
London W1D 5DU
020 7580 1974

GREAT DELIS

Lucy's Deli and 'Up The Duff' Pudding Club
Church Street
Ambleside
Cumbria LA22 0BU
01539 431191
www.lucysofambleside.co.uk

Cadogan & James Deli
31a The Square
Winchester
Hampshire SO23 9EX
01962 840805
www.jamesmartinchef.co.uk

Fenwick
Northumberland Street
Newcastle upon Tyne NE99 1AR
0191 232 5100
www.fenwick.co.uk/newcastle

Fanny's Farm Shop
Markedge Lane
Merstham
Redhill
Surrey RH1 3AW
01737 554444
www.fannysfarm.com

Partridges
2–5 Duke of York Square
London SW3 4LY
020 7730 0651
www.partridges.co.uk

GOOD-QUALITY CHOCOLATE AND SUGARCRAFT SUPPLIES

William Curley Chocolatier
10 Paved Court
Richmond upon Thames
Surrey TW9 1LZ
020 8332 3002
www.williamcurley.com

Chocolate Trading Company
Chorley Hall Lane
Alderley Edge
Cheshire SK9 7EU
01625 592808
www.chocolatetradingco.com

The Craft Company
Unit 6 and 7
Queens Park
Leamington Spa CV31 3LZ
01926 888507
www.craftcompany.co.uk

Imaginative Icing
22 Falsgrave Road
Scarborough
North Yorkshire YO12 5AT
01723 378116
www.imaginativeicing.co.uk